The
Web Wizard's
Guide to

Shockwave®

THE WEB WIZARD'S GUIDE TO SHOCKWAVE®

JAMES G. LENGEL

Addison
Wesley

Boston San Francisco New York
London Toronto Sydney Tokyo Singapore Madrid
Mexico City Munich Paris Cape Town Hong Kong Montreal

Executive Editor: *Susan Hartman Sullivan*
Project Editor: *Emily Genaway*
Associate Managing Editor: *Pat Mahtani*
Executive Marketing Manager: *Michael Hirsch*
Marketing Assistant: *Lesley Hershman*
Production Supervision: *Diane Freed*
Cover and Interior Designer: *Leslie Haimes*
Composition: *Gillian Hall, The Aardvark Group*
Copyeditor: *Chrysta Meadowbrooke*
Proofreader: *Holly McLean-Aldis*
Cover Design: *Gina Hagen Kolenda*
Prepress and Manufacturing: *Caroline Fell*

Access the latest information about Addison-Wesley titles from our World Wide
Web site: *http://www.aw.com/cs*

Many of the designations used by manufacturers and sellers to distinguish their
products are claimed as trademarks. Where those designations appear in this book,
and Addison-Wesley was aware of a trademark claim, the designations have been
printed in initial caps or all caps.

The programs and applications presented in this book have been included for their
instructional value. They have been tested with care, but are not guaranteed for
any particular purpose. The publisher does not offer any warranties or representa-
tions, not does it accept any liabilities with respect to the programs or applications.

Library of Congress Cataloging-in-Publication Data

Lengel, James G.
    The Web wizard's guide to Shockwave / James G. Lengel.
        p. cm.
    ISBN 0-321-12172-4
    1. Shockwave (Computer file) 2. Web sites--Design. 3. Interactive multimedia.
    I. Title.

    TK5105.8885.S56 L46 2003
    006.7'8769--dc21   2002074703

12345678910—QWT—040302

TABLE OF CONTENTS

PREFACE

About Addison-Wesley's Web Wizard Series

The beauty of the Web is that with a little effort, anyone can harness its power to create sophisticated Web sites. *Addison-Wesley's Web Wizard Series* helps readers master the Web by presenting a concise introduction to one important Internet topic or technology in each book. The books start from square one and assume no prior experience with the technology being covered. Mastering the Web doesn't come with a wave of a magic wand, but by studying these accessible, highly visual textbooks, readers will be well on their way.

The series is written by instructors familiar with the challenges that beginners face when first learning the material. To that end, the Web Wizard books offer more than a cookbook approach: they emphasize principles and offer clear explanations, giving the reader a strong foundation of knowledge on which to build.

Numerous features highlight important points and aid in learning:

☆ Tips—important points to keep in mind

☆ Shortcuts—time-saving ideas

☆ Warnings—things to watch out for

☆ Review questions and hands-on exercises

☆ On-line references—Web sites to visit for more information

Supplements

Supplementary materials for the books, including updates, additional examples, and source code, are available at `http://www.aw.com/webwizard`. Also available for instructors adopting a book from the series are instructors' manuals, test banks, PowerPoint slides, solutions, and Course Compass--a dynamic online course management system powered by Blackboard. Please contact your sales representative for the instructor resources access code.

About This Book

The Web Wizard's Guide to Shockwave gets you started designing and building an interactive project with rich media that can be made available over the Web. Shockwave projects are developed with Macromedia Director and published in the Web-friendly Shockwave file format.

Director is a powerful and flexible program that has been used for more than a decade to build interactive CD-ROM and Web projects. Its strengths are in animation; the incorporation of images, sound, and video; and user-initiated interactivity. This book will not cover all aspects of Director, but it will get you started and provide you with enough skills to build a simple Shockwave project.

This is a book for beginners, for people with experience in word-processing, graphics, and basic multimedia, but with little or no programming experience. As you work through the book, you will learn the possibilities of Shockwave, plan a Shockwave project, gather and prepare the materials you need, assemble them into Macromedia Director, program animation and interactivity, and, finally, publish the results to the Web.

At the College of Communication at Boston University, the hundreds of students who have taken *CM 523 Designing Interactive Communication* over the past eight years have inspired this book, and their process of learning is the basis of the approaches used in this book. The College Dean, Brent Baker, has provided during this time the encouragement and support that has made this work possible.

I am also indebted to the reviewers whose close reading and useful suggestions have greatly improved the usefulness of the chapters. My thanks go to Douglas Barkey, at the College of the Atlantic; Joseph Citta, of New York University; Dr. Karen L. Duda, from Youngstown State University; Kelly N. Fischbach, Ed. M., of Fablevision, Inc.; Sherry Hutson, at the University of Illinois, Springfield; Louise L. Soe, of California Polytechnic State University, Pomona; and James Wentworth, at the University of Colorado, Denver.

But the greatest inspiration and support for my work on this third book in the *Web Wizard* series comes from my family: Annie, Ben, Eileen, Kathi, Molly, and Murph, who encouraged me from the beginning and put up with a thousand inconveniences.

Jim Lengel
Boston, 2002

CHAPTER ONE

SHOCKWAVE: THE POSSIBILITIES

I'll rather keep
That which I have than, coveting for more,
be cast from possibility of all.
—from *Henry VI*

This chapter introduces you to what Shockwave can do and how it works, so you can prepare to create your own Shockwave content. The chapter begins with an examination of some of the very different ways that Web designers use Shockwave today, then goes on to explain the kinds of interactivity you can create. With Shockwave, the possibilities are unlimited: if you can imagine it, you can probably build it and deliver it on a Web site.

Chapter Objectives

☆ To examine exemplary Web sites that show the wide array of interactive possibilities you can deliver with Shockwave

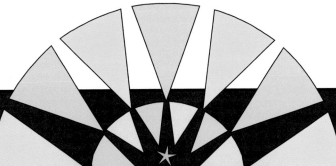

☆ To analyze Web interactivity according to nine key forms of user interaction with content

☆ To explore how Shockwave works on the Web and how you can create Shockwave movies with Macromedia Director

☆ To learn how Shockwave compares with other tools for creating interactive content and when it's best to use Shockwave

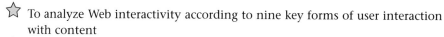 Examples of Shockwave on the Web

Shockwave is used for many different purposes on the Web. In many cases, you won't even know it's Shockwave. The best way to understand what Shockwave can do is to examine how it's being used on the Web today. Since the flat and static pages of this book cannot show interactivity, it's best to read this part of the chapter at your computer, connecting to each example and working through its interactivity. If you need more examples, you'll find them in the Online References section at the end of this chapter. The examples below demonstrate a wide range of Web activities created with Shockwave.

Timing Is Everything

The Timex watch company, eager to show off the myriad capabilities of its latest products, uses Shockwave to get its point across. What looks like a simple photo of the new Rush sport watch is actually a timepiece you can manipulate on the screen (Figure 1.1).

First of all, you notice that the watch is running with the correct time. Shockwave can pick up the actual date and time from the computer's clock and use them as part of the interactivity. If the time is not correct, you can reset the watch just as you would in the real world, by clicking and holding the SET•CLEAR button. Go to the site at `http://www.timex.com/flash/rushSIMULATION.html` and try it.

☆ **TIP**   **The Shockwave Plug-In**

You won't be able to see or work with the Timex watch, or with any other Shockwave example, unless your computer is equipped with the Shockwave player. This player comes built into the latest computers and browsers, so many people are all set. If you're not, you can download the player at `http://sdc.shockwave.com/shockwave/download/`.

Click the MODE•PULSE button to see the watch change to a timer, a stopwatch, an alarm clock, and a pulse meter. The START•STOP button at the top of the watch operates these modes. About the only thing you can't do with this virtual watch is take it off the screen and put it on your wrist. But there's a button at the bottom of the screen that lets you purchase the watch immediately, online.

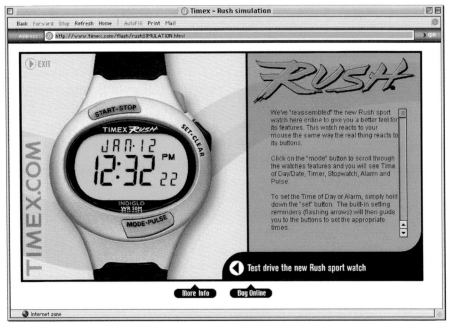

Figure 1.1 Interactive Simulation of the Timex Rush Sport Watch

This kind of interactive example is called a **simulation**, where the on-screen activity mimics the operation of something in the real world. The purpose of this simulation is to market and sell watches, a common form of communication on the Web. It uses several different types of interactivity:

☆ *Animation* of the time and date numbers and of pressing the control buttons on the watch

☆ *Manipulation*, as you click the buttons on the watch

☆ *Play*, as you try the various timings and settings of the watch and see the results

This example is also multimedia since it uses both image and sound in its interactivity: you can hear the watch announce its timings with a beep.

Timex chose Shockwave for this simulation because it could provide all of these forms of interactivity and could be developed quickly and easily. The same example could have been developed with Flash or as a Java applet, but not with the ease of Shockwave.

Dance to the Music

Milko the cow is the mascot for the Swedish food company of the same name. To help develop brand identity, Milko encourages its Web viewers to send its mascot on tour as a rock star, through a Shockwave example that lets you produce a music video (Figure 1.2). You can try it yourself at `http://farfar.2038.com/english/loader.html`.

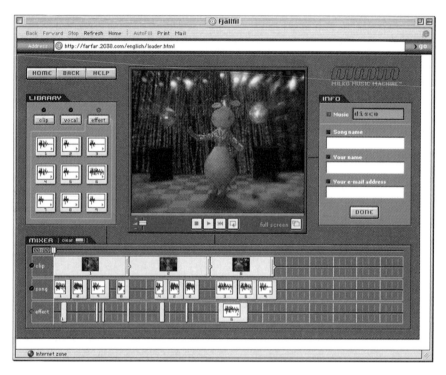

Figure 1.2 The Milko Music Machine

After learning about Milko's needs and interests through an animated story, you are taken to a control room where you can produce a music video with Milko as the star. By dragging video clips, song samples, and special effects into the timeline at the bottom, you create a unique multimedia experience that you can view in the window at the top. Shockwave can handle the multiple media types of this example—music, voice, video, and graphics—and integrate them into a unified and seamless online presentation that viewers can control.

This example is much more complex than the Timex watch and undoubtedly took more time to develop. It seems to achieve its purpose of keeping Web viewers involved with the company's name, and on its Web site, for a long time. This example uses several different types of interactivity:

☆ *Construction*, as you create an original music video from parts provided by the programmer

☆ *Manipulation*, as you drag and drop video and sound clips into the timeline

☆ *Animation*, as you watch Milko the cow speak, dance, sing, and cavort on stage

☆ *Play*, as you engage in an entertaining mix of creation and presentation that's responsive to your manipulations

Like the Timex watch, this example depends on interaction—nothing happens unless the user takes a series of actions that produce a responsive reaction from the computer. This action and reaction process is the essential motor of interactivity, which you will learn more about in the next section of this chapter. Shockwave's strength lies in its ability to produce these kinds of interactive exercises on the Web. In fact, the kind of multimedia interactivity in the Milko Music Machine would be almost impossible to produce with anything but Shockwave.

More Power to You

Along the south bank of the river Thames, the Battersea Power Station stands as an icon of the London skyline. No longer producing power, the station is being redeveloped as a business and entertainment complex. To sell its ideas to the public and potential tenants, the owners of the station have produced a Web site with Shockwave that includes many examples of online interactive multimedia public relations. You can see it at `http://www.thepowerstation.co.uk`.

This is a multidimensional site, designed to get people to think about the old power station in new ways. You can draw a picture of what the interior might look like. You can take a 3-D tour of the plans for the new station. You can play a pinball game. You can even create a virtual fireworks display at the power station overlooking the Thames. Music and sound effects accompany all these features. The static and silent pages of this book cannot communicate the interactivity of this site—you should experience it directly to understand it. All of the elements of this site were created with Shockwave. In fact, the items on the main menu of this site provide a succinct summary of what you can do with Shockwave: imagine, discover, create, escape, evolve, and play. At the Battersea site, you can:

☆ *Choose* which part of the site to interact with.

☆ *Animate* various parts of the station and related activities.

☆ *Play* within the scene and with the attached game.

Manage a Rain Forest

Rain forests are in the news as they succumb to the forces of economic development. To extend the public's understanding of this issue, MSNBC provides its online audience with an opportunity to manage a virtual rain forest as part of its Terminal Planet news series. Try it yourself at `http://www.msnbc.com/modules/rainforestSimulation/`.

Developed as a Shockwave project, this simulation lets you develop or conserve sections of the forest and then see how the results affect your profits as well as the number of species remaining (Figure 1.3). Develop too much and species disappear. Conserve too much and you go out of business.

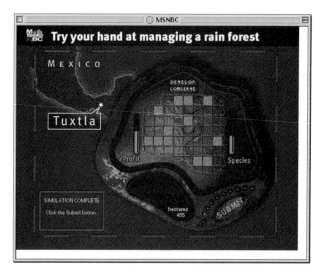

Figure 1.3 Managing a Rain Forest at MSNBC

In this example, the Shockwave developer programmed quite a bit of behind-the-scenes calculation, using mathematics to estimate the net profit from harvesting another 100 hectares of forest or to predict the decline in species based on the area of denuded countryside. The user never sees this math, but it is essential to the experience of managing the forest. Shockwave can perform quite an array of mathematical tasks and uses math throughout its operation. You need not be a mathematician to create a Shockwave project, but you do need to be ready to apply numbers and common formulas where necessary.

The interactivity in this example includes:

☆ *Choice*, of whether to develop or conserve and where in the forest to conduct your business

☆ *Animation*, as the results of your choices are displayed on the screen in the form of green and brown forest, along with moving graphs of profit and species count

☆ *Construction*, as you create an economic enterprise on the screen through your own choices

☆ *Play*, as you simulate decisions and reactions that in the real world would be impossible for most of us

The key to the success of this example is that you become aware of the results of your choices by the reactions they produce on the screen. Playing with the enterprise and interacting with complex material leads to better understanding. The company built the simulation with Shockwave because of its ability to handle graphics, mathematics, animation, and user feedback all at the same time, in a manner that allows rapid development.

⭐ **TIP**   **What Will You Build?**

For your first Shockwave project, a complex simulation such as managing the rain forest might be more than you can handle. Think about a smaller and less complex project that nonetheless employs the varied kinds of interactivity you have seen in the examples so far. In Chapter Two, you'll begin planning and constructing a project of your own.

Other Examples

The four examples above do not exhaust the possibilities of Shockwave. Here are some others you should review, analyzing each for the kinds of interactivity involved.

☆ The Glenn Gould Performance Database (`http://www.multimediali-brary.com/Music/Gould/Gould.html`). This shows Shockwave used as an interactive database that helps music fans find all of the performances of this famed pianist. Search by year, composer, country, composition, or conductor, and see immediate results. This is a great example of search and find interactivity.

☆ Jimmy McPartland's Jazz (`http://www.multimedialibrary.com/Music/Jimmy.html`). On the same site as the Glenn Gould example, you can listen to music by departed cornetist Jimmy McPartland with a Shockwave music player. Stop, start, and adjust the volume as the video streams to you in real time.

☆ Mr. Hankey (`http://www.comedycentral.com/southparkgames/playset/`). Though it borders on bad taste, this unique Shockwave example teaches you about South Park's Mr. Hankey with a multimedia slide show, then lets you build your own Mr. Hankey in a virtual environment similar to Mr. Potato Head. Manipulation and construction are the chief forms of interactivity here.

☆ Fat Boy Raids the Cookie Factory (`http://www.shockwave.com/bin/content/shockwave.jsp?id=cookiefactory`). A mindless entertainment, perhaps, but it shows how Shockwave can be used to create something like a video game. Manipulate the fat boy through the cookie factory; he eats morsels as he avoids dangers.

☆ The Secret of Sherwood (`http://www.maidmarian.com/Sherwood.htm`). This three-dimensional avatar chart room, constructed with Shockwave, shows two advanced features: the multiuser server and 3-D graphics, which enable Shockwave examples to move beyond the flat screen and the single user. The animation and manipulation in this example are its chief forms of interactivity.

These examples show some of the possibilities of Shockwave. They show the many different types of media—text, numbers, images, sound, music, video, and

☆ **SHORTCUT More Examples**

You'll find leads to more online Shockwave examples at the Macromedia Showcase, Shockwave.com, and DirectorWeb, whose URLs appear in the Online References section at the end of this chapter.

3-D effects—that Shockwave can handle. They show many of the purposes that interactivity can achieve on the Web, from education to entertainment to marketing. And they show the many different kinds of organizations that are using Shockwave to build online experiences for their audiences.

But why did all these folks choose Shockwave to develop their examples? Why didn't they use other Web development tools, such as HTML, JavaScript, Java applets, or Flash? After all, HTML requires no plug-in and is easy to develop. JavaScript can work without a plug-in and downloads in an instant. Flash can animate better, with less overhead and faster download. A Java applet can display without a plug-in. So why did these examples use Shockwave? The answer lies in Shockwave's ease of development and possibilities for interactivity. In the next section you'll learn more about the various kinds of interactivity that people can experience on a Web site.

☆ **WARNING More Than Shockwave**

Using Shockwave is not the only way to develop interactivity on the Web: JavaScript, Java applets, Flash, CGI scripts, Active Server Pages, and other technologies can accomplish the same goals. This book concentrates on those forms of interactivity for which Shockwave is best. Other books in the Web Wizard series can help you build interactivity with the other tools.

◎◎ Nine Forms of Interactivity

Interactivity. It's what distinguishes the new media from the old. It's what makes communication responsive and personal. We want to build Web sites that interact with the user. Everybody talks about interactivity, but few have defined it.

At its simplest, an interactive work involves action on the part of the user (or viewer, or reader, or player), which provokes another action on the part of the computer. And vice versa.

Interactivity comes in many forms. During an interactive Web experience, you can choose, animate, search and find, buy and sell, manipulate, construct, question, converse, and play.

Choose

You can select the place you want to visit or the topic you want to explore. You can click on the word you want to know more about or choose the city you want to fly to. Choosing is the simplest form of interactivity. Choice is inherent in the structure of the World Wide Web and is included in the simplest Web sites. When you make your choice, something happens: you are taken to the story you chose, or you see your avatar turn around on the screen, or you see your profits slide.

Animate

You can click to see a process in action, illustrate a concept with a moving diagram, or watch an event occur over time and space. Animations on demand can provide the ideas when you need them in the form most appropriate to their understanding. When animation is combined with manipulation (see below), the result is even more interactive. On the Biology Place Web site, (`http://www. biology.com`) for instance, you can learn about the process of cell division by manipulating an animation of typical cells.

Search and Find

Any time we can let the computer help us find what we're looking for, it seems more interactive. A multidimensional menu is a simple form of searching and finding. Searching by key word and then choosing from a list of hits is perhaps a bit more interactive. The more open and natural the search method, and the more it can find things that would be hard to find otherwise, the more interactive it seems.

Buy and Sell

Making a commercial transaction—renting a car, buying a book, and subscribing to a magazine—is an essential interaction between buyer and seller. As the Web expands its commercial potential, this form of interactivity proliferates. The more direct and quick and responsive the transaction, the more you will perceive it as interactive. When buying and selling is combined with searching, finding, and choosing (see above), the result can be substantially more effective.

Manipulate

Moving things around on the screen with the mouse is a viscerally interactive process. It allows you to make complex selections and to see immediately the results of your choices. It gives the feeling that you are controlling the computer and not just reacting to it. To provide the feel of interactivity, this manipulation must be more than the "joystick" controls found in computer action and Nintendo games; it must be direct and visible.

Construct

In this higher form of manipulation you build something on the screen by making choices, manipulating objects, and selecting alternatives. The results take shape on the page as you build your construction; they may even take action based on the nature of the build. This most complex form of interactivity puts you in the role of author, a complete about-face.

Question

Asking an expert, and getting a response immediately, or later through email, is a satisfying and very human process. Question and answer systems are a way to extend the function of a new media product to better fit the exact needs of an individual user. The answers to these questions need not be delivered by a live and listening respondent; rather, the program must convince the user that her questions are indeed being answered.

Converse

Talk is the natural form of interaction for the human species. Conversation is what makes the telephone and email the most popular interactive technologies. Conversation can happen on a Web site in synchronous (chat rooms) or asynchronous (threaded discussions) forms of conversation among its users. Conversation can also be simulated, through Shockwave projects that parse the user's entries and respond based on a database of terms and some simple logic.

Play

The Swiss developmental psychologist Jean Piaget believed that it's through the interaction of play that we build our intellectual capacities. All of the forms of interaction listed above can include a component of play. Playing with objects or ideas or people is a good way to get to know them. Play may be the highest form of interactivity.

Shockwave and Interactivity

Few Shockwave projects include all the forms of interactivity described above. But since this chapter is about the possibilities of Shockwave, it's a good idea to think widely at the outset, to consider all the ways that communication on the Web can be a two-way street between the user and the content. This book shows you the tools and skills necessary to build these kinds of interactivity at a beginner's level. It's up to you to apply these techniques to your own interactive project as you go along.

◎◎ How Shockwave Works

Shockwave is not a software program that you purchase in a shrink-wrapped box as you would Dreamweaver, Flash, or Microsoft Office. Rather, it's a system for developing, delivering, and viewing interactive multimedia content for the Web. You develop Shockwave projects with an application called **Macromedia Director Shockwave Studio**, referred to from here on simply as **Director**. Director creates files in its own format, with the filename extension `.dir`. You save your completed project onto a Web server in what is called the Shockwave format, with a `.dcr` filename extension. This file is in most cases embedded in a Web page with HTML. When a member of your audience opens that page with a Web browser, the Shockwave file is handled by a plug-in called **Shockwave Player** (sometimes called the Shockwave Plug-in) and displayed on the screen for the user to interact with.

Shockwave and Director

To build your own Shockwave projects, you need a copy of Director on your computer. This book uses Director version 8.5, so you will need that or a higher version to follow the instructions properly. Director is published by Macromedia, Inc., the same company that publishes Dreamweaver, Flash, FreeHand, SoundEdit, and other professional multimedia development tools. Director is a **development**

environment: a set of software tools that enables you to build interactive multi-media content.

☆ **WARNING** Versions of Director

The illustrations in this book and the step-by-step instructions were developed with Director 8.5. But most of the tasks can be accomplished identically with Director 8. Director 7 lacks the Property Inspector and other features used in this book.

Director can *import* almost any kind of digital media: text, bitmapped images, vector graphics, sound, video, animation, and others. It can read most common formats for these media, from Joint Photographic Experts Group (JPEG) to QuickTime, from Audio Interchange File Format (AIFF) to Flash. It can read them from almost any place on the Web. And it can display them to users on the Web, singly or in combination.

Director can also *control* these media as they are presented. Director lets you (or the user) control when, where, how big, how long, and how loud or how bright each morsel of media appears on the screen. It lets you direct these media, to play the role of director in the production you are building.

Finally, Director lets you program these media objects so that they *interact* with the user (and with each other and with time and space), such that when something happens, the project responds in a certain way.

As a Shockwave developer using Director, you import media, control its display over time and space, and program any necessary interactivity until you have a project that works the way you want. Director lets you build and test the project at the same time. After extensive testing, you use Director to publish the project as a Shockwave file. This `.dcr` file is a compressed version of the standard Director (`.dir`) file. This `.dcr` Shockwave file is copied to the Web server and sent to the audience.

Shockwave on the Web

In most cases, the Shockwave file is embedded in or linked to from a standard HTML Web page. When the user's Web browser encounters the Shockwave file, it calls on the Shockwave Player to handle the display of the project. The Shockwave Player downloads or streams the file from the Web server to the user's computer and displays it on the screen (and/or plays it through the speakers). Without the Shockwave Player, the user cannot see, hear, or interact with the Shockwave content.

According to Macromedia, more than 165 million users have the Shockwave Player installed, and 200,000 more install it each day. The Player is also distributed widely by computer and software vendors. According to a Shockwave white paper from Macromedia, Inc. (see the Online References section):

☆ Every Macintosh with System 8 or higher has Shockwave Player preinstalled.

☆ All copies of Microsoft Windows 95/98 and Windows 2000 distributed to PC manufacturers include the Shockwave Player, allowing it to be preinstalled on every Windows PC.

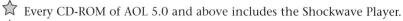

☆ Every CD-ROM of AOL 5.0 and above includes the Shockwave Player.

☆ Every CD-ROM of Microsoft Internet Explorer 4 and above includes the Shockwave Player.

☆ The Personal Edition CD for Netscape Navigator 4 and above has the Shockwave Player. The Communicator Update Web page installs the Shockwave Player.

☆ Users can download Shockwave Player for free from `http://www.macromedia.com` and `http://www.shockwave.com`.

☆ Macromedia offers Web publishers free licensing to distribute the Shockwave Player on their intranets, on CD/DVD-ROMs, and on the Internet within another application.

The Shockwave Player provides the code that allows computers to process the interactivity inherent in the Shockwave project. The diagram in Figure 1.4 shows how Director, the Shockwave file, the Web server, the user's Web browser, and the Shockwave Player work together to allow development and distribution of Shockwave content.

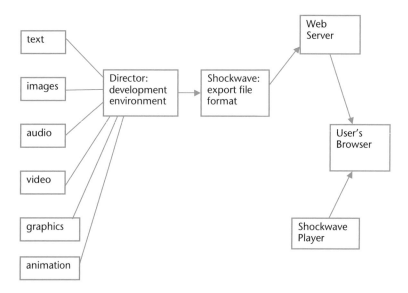

Figure 1.4 Shockwave Development and Distribution Diagram

Lingo and Interactivity

Many programs enable you to display multimedia content on a Web page: HTML can show text and images, while QuickTime, RealPlayer, and Windows Media Player can show video and play sound. And most Web-page editors such as

Dreamweaver and FrontPage make it easy for novices to include such media in their Web pages. But few programs enable you to place *interactive* content on the Web, media that the user can move, manipulate, animate, control, and respond to. The feature of Shockwave that the others lack is a scripting language called **Lingo**.

A **scripting language** lets you write little programs that respond to user activity. Suppose you create a simple sailboat simulation in which the user must move the boat past the rocks without hitting them. The screen might look like Figure 1.5.

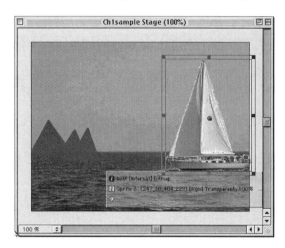

Figure 1.5 Sample Sailboat Simulation

In Director, each object you can see on the screen is called a **sprite**. The boat is sprite 3, and the rock is sprite 4. If the boat hits the rock, the player hears a crunching sound, loses a point, and sees the boat sink. The script that senses and responds to the boat striking the rock might look like this:

```
if sprite 3 intersects sprite 4 then
    puppetsound 1, "crunch"
    score = score -1
    go to "sinking boat"
end if
```

☆ **TIP** **Scripts**

Don't worry if this script makes no sense to you right now—it's here just to illustrate the nature of Lingo. In Chapter Five you will learn how scripts work and how to write your own.

This script was composed in Director using its Lingo scripting language, which is like a programming language but closer to plain English and a bit less formal than C++ or Java. But its open-ended structure allows you to create many forms of complex interactivity. The first line of the script—`if sprite 3 intersects sprite 4`—senses, or **traps**, the event of the boat hitting the rock. If indeed these two objects intersect, three things happen:

1. The crunching sound is played through the speakers: `puppetsound 1, "crunch"`.

2. The score is decremented by 1 point: `score = score -1`.

3. The movie advances to an animation where the boat sinks:
   `go to "sinking boat"`.

This is the essence of interactivity: responding to the user's actions with an appropriate result. The Lingo script makes the interactivity work. Without Lingo and scripts like these, Shockwave would simply be a tool for displaying multimedia content on a Web page. It's Lingo that enables interactivity. Later in this book you will learn how to write simple Lingo scripts to create basic interactivity for your Shockwave projects.

Director provides you the tools to compose and test Lingo scripts in your project. The Shockwave Player contains the code that interprets and responds to the scripts sent to it by the Shockwave file. All of these work together to produce an interactive experience for your audience.

Working with Director

You will use Director to build your Shockwave project. The process for using Director follows the steps given below, each of which is expanded in subsequent chapters of this book. This list is included here to give you an idea of where you are heading.

1. *Set your goals.*

   a. Determine the ideas you want to communicate, the nature of your audience, and the kind of interactivity you need to achieve your purpose with that audience.

2. *Plan the project.*

   a. Sketch the flow of the work. What will the user see? In what order? What choices will they have? In most cases, a flow chart is the best way to make this sketch, but a script, a screenplay, or a storyboard may work just as well.

   b. Sketch out the design of each main screen or scene in your project. Assign a short name to each of these.

   c. List the elements needed for each scene. These should include, as necessary, photographs, drawings, diagrams, music, voice, video, text, and buttons.

3. *Import cast members.*

   a. Develop each element in your list, and save it in a project folder on the hard disk of your computer. Use whatever image-, sound-, text- or video-editing programs you need to compose each element. Adjust the size of each element to fit the way it's going to be used. Save each element in a proper format.

b. Open Director. Set up your Score, Cast, Tools, and Control Panel windows in convenient places.

c. Import each element into the Cast window (Figure 1.6).

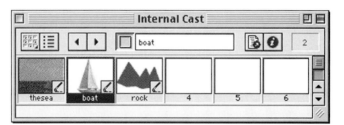

Figure 1.6 Cast Members in Director's Cast Window

4. Build the score.

a. Create markers in the Score window. With your sketch (from step 2) as a guide, put markers in the Score window, each with a short name. The markers will set forth the basic structure of your project. Each scene should have a marker, and many scenes will have additional markers within them.

b. Place cast members into the Score window by dragging them from the Cast window onto the Stage window. Put background elements into the first channels, foreground elements into later channels. Place stationary elements first, then place any animated elements. Make sure you place them in the Score window in accordance with your markers. Sounds go in the sound channels at the top; everything else goes in the sprite channels below.

c. Build one scene at a time. Start by placing elements into a single frame. Then copy them across the scene as appropriate. Expand the length of a scene as necessary by inserting new frames. Markers will move accordingly.

d. Test each scene. Place the playback head (in the Score window) at the beginning of the scene. Move the Cast, Score, and Tools windows aside. Then use the Control Panel to move forward manually frame by frame. Adjust the score as necessary until the scene plays correctly. Test often as you compose.

5. Add stops, transitions, timing, and loops.

a. Create the visual effects you want by adding transitions in the transition channel. Transitions go into the frame where the change occurs.

b. Make the program pause at the end of a scene (if necessary) by writing a "go to the frame" script in the script channel.

c. In the timing channel, you may need to instruct the program to wait for movies or sounds to finish.

d. To make a loop, write a "go to <marker>" script in the script channel.

6. Add buttons and interactive elements.

a. Place button cast members into the score by dragging them in from the Cast window onto the Stage.

b. Write a script for each button as necessary.

7. Test your project.

a. Move the Score, Tools, and Cast windows aside. Use the Control Panel to play your movie.

b. Interact with the movie as it plays. Make notes on what doesn't work right.

c. Move the Score window back into place, and adjust as necessary.

d. Repeat steps a through c until everything works correctly or until you go bonkers, whichever comes first.

8. Show your project to others.

a. Let them use it for a bit, then ask for their suggestions for improvement.

b. Show the project to your instructor or supervisor, asking again for suggestions.

c. Go back and improve it until you are satisfied.

9. Publish your project in Shockwave format.

a. Save the Shockwave file to your hard disk.

b. Embed the Shockwave file in a Web page.

c. Test the Web page with Microsoft Internet Explorer and Netscape Navigator.

d. Revise as necessary.

10. Publish your project on the Web.

a. Copy your Web page and Shockwave file to a Web server.

b. Connect to your Web page with both browsers and test again.

The remainder of this book will take you step-by-step through this process, with detailed instructions along the way.

◎◎ When to Use Shockwave

Shockwave is a rich and versatile Web development environment, but it's not the best way to do everything you might want to accomplish on a Web site. While Shockwave can handle all the forms of interactivity described earlier in this chapter, there are other development tools that may be better suited to certain objectives. Shockwave's unique strength lies in developing complex interactivity in rich media environments—Shockwave does that very well—but there are times when another tool will suit you better. And because viewing Shockwave content requires a plug-in, Shockwave may not be the best choice for certain novice or low-power audiences. This section of the chapter explains Shockwave's strengths and weaknesses in each of the forms of interactivity, then goes on to set forth some general guidelines on when to use Shockwave and when to avoid it.

Choose

You can build all kinds of choice-type interactivity with Shockwave, from animated rollover navigation buttons that show the user a new page to a pop-up menu list of choices for selecting products. But for simple pages on which the viewer chooses from a simple list of choices, Shockwave is not necessary. You can construct a simple choice list in HTML; you can create a set of buttons or a pop-up menu with a WYSIWYG Web-page editor such as Dreamweaver. These methods allow users to make simple choices without the necessity of a plug-in or the complexity of creating a Shockwave project.

Other kinds of complex choices (for example, when previous choices must be remembered from screen to screen; when choices are dragged and dropped on the page; when choices are best made through graphics; when mathematical calculations of different variables help determine the choices) call for development with Shockwave. Shockwave's built-in behaviors and extensible Lingo scripting language, along with its plethora of mathematical operators and functions, allow you to create and present different methods for choice making.

Animate

Quick-moving vector graphic animations are best developed in Flash, while simple bitmap animation can be built with GIFBuilder or Photoshop. If animation is all you need, you don't need Shockwave. Shockwave makes it easy to build these kinds of animations, but it needs a large plug-in to make it work. The other methods work with a smaller plug-in (Flash) or no plug in at all (GIF). But when the animation involves moving objects that interact with each other or with the user, and if they are bitmaps rather than vector shapes, then Shockwave may be the best tool for development and delivery.

Director began as an animation program. Later other features were added, but at its heart it is a tool for making objects move across the screen over time and putting that movement under user control.

Search and Find

For searching large databases of information, Shockwave alone cannot do the job. This kind of interactivity requires a Web page linked to a server-side database. But for small collections of information, Shockwave can perform simple searches and return the information quickly, without resorting to a server. The data to be searched is included in the Shockwave file or made available on the Web; you use a Shockwave graphic interface and Lingo scripting to examine the data and then to present the results to the viewer. These kinds of searches are fast because they do not require communication with or processing by a server—all the work is done on the viewer's computer.

Shockwave can also serve as the front end of a server-based search-and-find system: the user forms his or her search strategy on a screen with Shockwave's graphic and interactive possibilities, which generate a search command that Shockwave sends to the server over the Web. This allows you to combine the flexibility and multimedia possibilities of Shockwave with the search capability of a large database.

Buy and Sell

Shockwave is not an e-commerce development environment. Buying and selling online requires linked databases of customers, products, and payments, all linked to secure transaction and credit agencies. Shockwave cannot build these kinds of applications. But it can help get the customer ready to buy, as in the Timex watch example at the beginning of this chapter. With Shockwave you can also build interactive "dress the model" or "build the car" examples in which the customer can manipulate clothing, colors, accessories, or objects right on the computer screen and see the results as if he or she were in the store. Shockwave can also help you build simple pricing calculators and estimators.

Manipulate

This is where Shockwave has clear advantages over other development environments. Moving objects around the screen, dragging and dropping, and other manipulative user interactivity is easy to do in Shockwave. Shockwave provides built-in behaviors for such functions. You can build this kind of interactivity with Flash, but not as easily; to build such applications as Java applets would require extensive time and sophisticated programming skills. Neither JavaScript nor HTML nor database programming can provide users of your project with this kind of manipulation.

Construct

To show the results of construction—a watch, a car, a building—you don't need to use Shockwave. Instead, place a high-quality photo on the Web page, or create a virtual reality panorama in QuickTime. The simple presentation of items is best done with these noninteractive technologies. But if you want to involve the user in the act of constructing—to let her or him build something new from a set of objects on the screen and to do it in a way that mimics construction in the real world—then Shockwave is the best choice. It's easier to develop such functionality in Shockwave than in Flash or Java, the only other realistic options.

Question and Converse

Two kinds of question-and-answer functions are often seen on the Web—**chat rooms** where one person poses a question and others respond and **information finders** such as Ask Jeeves that parse a user's question and respond with a list of possible answers. In most cases, chat rooms are built with proprietary server-based chat software licensed to the Web publisher. Proven workhorses that have already been built are AOL Instant Messenger and WebEx. Information finders in most cases involve text parsing and matching programs that run on the server, such as the examples designed by Artificial Life. Neither Flash nor Java nor JavaScript nor HTML would be very good at developing this kind of question-and-answer functionality.

But you can use Shockwave to develop both chat rooms and information finders in a simple way. The Shockwave multiuser server lets different users, each working in their own Shockwave movie, send and receive messages to and from each other over the Web, and so it can be used to build your own chat or discussion. Shockwave also contains built-in tools for searching strings of text and for finding and counting words in a passage, which is necessary for the information-finder type of interactivity. You can see an example of such an application built with Shockwave at `http://www.aw.com/webwizard`, click on "Multimedia", then "Ask the Wizard".

Play

To create playful, gamelike experiences on the Web, you could build use Java, Virtual Reality Markup Language (VRML), Flash, or Shockwave. Java and VRML require building everything from scratch, call for serious programming skill, and take a lot of work—and the results will not work uniformly on all browsers and all platforms. Flash may work best to develop simple playlike interaction that's based on vector animation and limited interactivity. Shockwave is the best choice for building highly interactive playful experiences with rich media resources. And it works well across platforms and browsers. Many of the examples mentioned in this chapter exploit the interactivity of play in a variety of ways. And all were built with Shockwave.

Shockwave versus Flash

Probably the closest competitor to Shockwave these days is Macromedia Flash. Flash in some ways looks and feels like Director and can be used to create some of the same content. There's no clear line separating the two when it comes to developing interactivity, but Table 1.1 shows a set of continua between them.

Macromedia publishes on its Web site a quick comparison of its two leading development tools (see the URL in the *Online References* section).

Table 1.1 Shockwave versus Flash

	Shockwave	Flash
Content	Works well with all forms of multimedia: text, video, photos, 3-D effects, music, voice, and Flash animations	Works best with vector graphics, text, and sound
Publishing	Works best with Web, CD-ROM, and DVD formats	Works best with Web format
Development tools	Covers all media and all forms of interactivity; extensive and extensible	Concentrates on vector graphics and text animation with some interactivity
Plug-in	Is large in size, with 75% installed base	Is small in size, with 90% installed base
Interactivity	Provides all kinds, plus Web-based multiuser functionality	Works best for click and choose interactivity

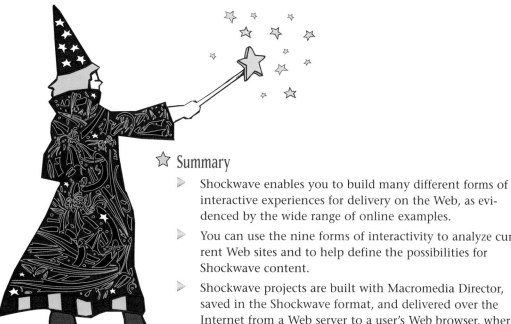

☆ Summary

▷ Shockwave enables you to build many different forms of interactive experiences for delivery on the Web, as evidenced by the wide range of online examples.

▷ You can use the nine forms of interactivity to analyze current Web sites and to help define the possibilities for Shockwave content.

▷ Shockwave projects are built with Macromedia Director, saved in the Shockwave format, and delivered over the Internet from a Web server to a user's Web browser, where the Shockwave Player handles the playback. The built-in Lingo scripting language makes possible complex interactivity including media from many sources.

▷ Shockwave is not always the best tool for building interactivity. Its strengths lie in combining rich media resources with complex interactivity.

☆ Online References

Collections of Shockwave projects:

Macromedia Showcase
http://www.macromedia.com/showcase/

Shockwave.com
http://www.shockwave.com/sw/home/

DirectorWeb
http://hakatai.mcli.dist.maricopa.edu/director/
shockwave.html

Shockwave versus Flash comparison
http://www.macromedia.com/
software/director/resources/integration/flash/

Shockwave White Paper
http://www.macromedia.com/software/
director/whitepapers/

Shockwave Resource Center
http://www.macromedia.com/software/director/resources/
integration/

☆Review Questions

1. What possibilities does Shockwave offer that are not available with other Web media systems?

2. For each example described at the beginning of this chapter, identify the intended audience for the project, and rate the example's effectiveness.

3. How can a Web user acquire the Shockwave Player?

4. Explain three different forms of interactivity that you can build with Director and deliver with Shockwave. Give an example of each.

5. What is the role of the Lingo scripting language in Director?

6. List the steps in the process of building a Shockwave project.

7. Explain the differences between Shockwave and Flash, with examples of the strengths of each.

☆Hands-On Exercises

1. Using the resources and online references supplied in this chapter, find and work through Shockwave projects on the Web that illustrate at least five of the forms of interactivity described in this chapter.

2. Find six friends or acquaintances and determine whether or not they have the Shockwave Player on their computer. For those who do not, assist them in downloading the current version and testing it with one of the example projects listed in this chapter.

3. Download the sailboat simulation file from the Shockwave section of the Web Wizard Web site. Open the sailboat simulation file with Director. Play it. Then open the Script window and examine the script shown in this chapter.

4. Go to the Flash showcase at the Macromedia Web site. Examine two examples of Flash projects, and compare them with the Shockwave projects you viewed in this chapter.

5. Describe in two paragraphs a project of your own that you could build with Director and publish in Shockwave format. Keep it simple, but include at least three of the forms of interactivity mentioned in this chapter.

CHAPTER TWO

THE SHOCKWAVE DEVELOPMENT ENVIRONMENT

*All the world's a stage,
and all the men and women merely players.
They have their exits and their entrances;
And one man in his time plays many parts.*

—from *As You Like It*

If you have never used Macromedia Director, you will find it an unusual program. It sets up an environment for the creation of interactive projects that is unlike most other computer applications. This chapter introduces the Shockwave development environment and gets you started creating a simple Shockwave example. Most importantly, it introduces the *theater* metaphor that is essential to Director. To be successful as a Shockwave developer, you must learn to think in terms of putting on a show in a theater, where you play the role of director of the production, as well as the playwright and producer.

Chapter Objectives

☆ To understand Director's various windows and how you can use them to develop a Shockwave project

☆ To learn about the different types of media that Director can use and how they fit into the programming environment

☆ To understand the role of time, frames, and sprites in Director's Score

☆ To see how animation works in the director Score and Stage, combining time and space

☆ To understand how Lingo scripts can create interactivity

☆ To create a simple production using Director

◎◎ Director's Stage, Cast, and Score

Imagine that you are the director of a theater production—a play on the stage. The play is *Hamlet*, by William Shakespeare. The scene takes place in the graveyard, where Hamlet contemplates the skull of Yorick.

> *Alas, poor Yorick! I knew him, Horatio; a fellow of infinite jest,*
> *of most excellent fancy.*
>
> —*Hamlet*, Act V, Scene 1

What do you need to consider as you prepare and direct this scene? You need first to think about the setting: the stage on which you will place the action and the backdrop and scenery put on the stage. Then you need to think about the actors who will form the cast that acts out the scene, along with the props they hold. Of course, you need copies of the scripts, which tell each actor what to say and do. And then you need to decide where to place the cast members and how to move them as they deliver their lines. Your plan might look like Table 2.1.

Table 2.1 Items Needed to Produce Hamlet

Category	Item
Stage	Graveyard backdrop
Cast	Hamlet, Horatio, Gravedigger
Props	Skull, shovel, dirt
Script	Words and actions for Hamlet
Audio	Wind blowing ominously

Developing a Shockwave project is like putting on a play. And the Director software uses the metaphor of a theater in its workings.

Figure 2.1 shows the essential windows in the Director programming environment: the Stage, the Cast, the Score, the Control Panel, and the Tool Palette. They are empty—the actors have not arrived, the backdrop is yet to be painted, and the

Director's Stage, Cast, and Score

script is unopened. Building a Shockwave project involves filling these windows with media and information in such a way that they create the interactive experience you want on your Web site.

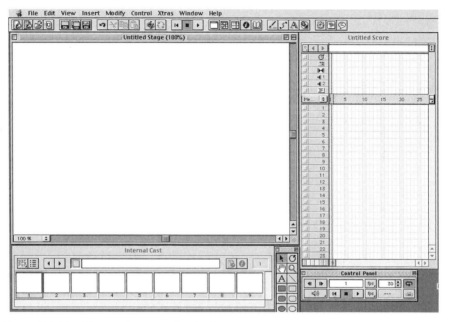

Figure 2.1 The Director Programming Environment

The Stage

The main window in the Director programming environment is called the **Stage**. This is where the action takes place, the play is performed, and the interaction is pursued. The Stage is the only window that the audience sees—the rest are backstage, visible only to the director.

The Cast

The window at the bottom left is called the **Cast**. This is where all the items that make up your project are stored as they wait to appear on the Stage. Think of the Cast as a set of chairs placed backstage out of sight of the audience but close to

☆ **SHORTCUT Window Placement**

You can move Director's windows around the screen and place them wherever you want. The ones you see in Figure 2.1 are just the five essential windows—there are dozens more you could open as you need them. Windows can overlap, which can make the screen confusing and hard to work with. Throughout this book, you will see the essential windows arranged as in Figure 2.1, without overlaps and in these same positions. Positioning the windows in a consistent arrangement, without overlaps, makes your development easier.

the director. Before the play can begin, all the cast members must be assembled in their chairs, ready to go onto the stage on cue, at the proper time. All the media in your project will show up in the Cast window—images, sounds, text, video, even backgrounds and scripts. A typical Shockwave project may involve over 100 cast members.

The Score

The **Score** is the most important window for the developer. With this window we mix the metaphor just a bit, bringing in a device used by musical composers and conductors to arrange the various parts in a symphony or opera. On a musical score, each instrument's part is shown across one line, and the notes proceed from left to right over time (Figure 2.2). In this way, the composer and conductor can see all the instruments that are playing (and those that are silent) at any moment in time.

The Score window in Director is like this musical score. It shows the developer which cast member is doing what at each point in time. Like the instruments, each cast member on the Stage has its own line across the Score. The Score also shows the tempo of the playback, just like the musical score, and as the Director movie plays, the action moves across the Score from left to right as time passes. One note in the music is like one frame in the Director Score. While the conductor would turn the pages in the score as the symphony proceeds, the Shockwave developer simply scrolls the Score window.

The Control Panel

In rehearsal, the conductor starts the musicians with a click of her or his baton, lets them play for a while, and then stops the action as necessary to perfect the technique. The **Control Panel** in Director accomplishes this task. By clicking the play button, you can start the action, watch it proceed, stop it, go back, and play it again. This kind of manipulation is an important part of the project development. The Control Panel also permits you to move forward or back one frame (one note in the musical score) at a time. The Control Panel also shows the tempo of the piece in two ways: (1) the tempo (in frames per second) that you set and (2) the tempo that the movie is actually playing, which may be different. Just as musicians may not be able to keep up with a quick tempo set by a composer, the cast members in a Director movie cannot always move and perform their scripts as fast as the developer intended. This difference in tempos is displayed in the Control Panel.

The Tool Palette

The **Tool Palette** is like the inkwell of the musical composer. As a Shockwave developer, you can dip into the Tool Palette for a tool that will let you paint a certain kind of cast member onto the Stage. It's similar in function to the Tool Palette in Adobe Photoshop—you click a tool to select it, then click and drag the pointer across the Stage to draw the item. There are tools to select, zoom, rotate, or move items on the Stage; tools to create text, shapes, lines, buttons, and check boxes; and tools to choose foreground and background colors.

Figure 2.2 A Musical Score

Coordinated Windows

All the windows work together. As the items are drawn on the Stage, they are auto-matically entered into the Cast window and into the Score. You can drag a cast member from the Cast onto the Stage, and it will automatically appear in the Score. If you delete a member from its place in the Score, it will disappear from the Stage as well—and vice versa.

> ☆ **TIP**   **For Flash Users**
>
> If you are familiar with the windows in the Flash programming environment, you will see that Flash's Timeline is similar to (but not exactly the same as) Director's Score and that the Stage serves the same purpose in both, as does the Control Panel and the Tool Palette. The closest thing to Director's Cast window is the Flash Library.

It is in these essential windows that you compose your masterpiece. By setting up, seeing, and testing cast members with these five windows, you create the ani-mation and interactivity that can bring new capabilities to Web sites.

◎◉ Actors: Text, Images, Sound, Music, Video

Shockwave projects can include all kinds of content—long passages of text, photo-graphs, drawings, animations, music, voice, sound effects, and video—even virtual reality panoramas. This means that the Cast window can contain many different kinds of characters, all of whom can display on the Stage and be heard or seen by the audience. No matter what form of media they appear in, all of these elements are called **cast members** in the Director environment, and they all show up in the Cast window. Shockwave is the only system for combining rich media of so many different types into a coordinated, interactive whole.

Preparing the Elements

Before assembling the Shockwave project in Director, you must prepare each of these media elements individually, in most cases by using specialized software pro-grams such as Photoshop (for images), Flash (for vector animations), SoundEdit (for audio), or Final Cut Pro (for video). Chapter Three of this book provides details on preparing each type of media element. Once prepared, the elements are import-ed into Director's Cast window (Figure 2.3). From the Cast, you drag them to the Stage and the Score as necessary to arrange the action. Then you adjust, script, and animate them to make the production come to life.

While Director includes a set of painting tools and a text editor that can help create and edit images and text once they are imported, most media for a Shockwave project must be edited outside Director, using the more appropriate editing software mentioned above. Once elements are imported, Director can do little (except for images and text) to change how they look or sound. So you'll find yourself spending considerable time, especially at the beginning of a project, enmeshed in the various media editing and preparation programs. Table 2.2 shows some of these programs and which media they help edit.

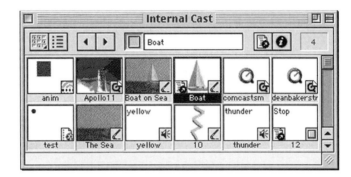

Figure 2.3 A Typical Cast Window Full of Elements

Table 2.2 Software Programs for Editing Media

Media	Software
Text	Word
Images	Photoshop, Illustrator
Animation	Flash, Fireworks, GIFBuilder
Audio	SoundEdit, SoundForge
Video	iMovie, Premiere, Final Cut Pro

The Shockwave developer works like a theater director who must prepare the actors before they are ready for the stage, spending time with them practicing their lines, correcting their diction, and sewing their costumes. Depending on the number of cast members and their condition at the outset, this can take quite a bit of energy and often calls for significant expertise. But good actors, well prepared, are essential to a successful performance. So it may take some time to fill the Cast window with well-prepared media elements.

Time: Frames, Scenes, Movies, and Markers

A play in the theater opens with the curtain, followed a few seconds later by the entrance of the first actor, who delivers his or her lines interspersed with carefully timed pauses. More minutes and lines and entrances proceed through time, until the end of the first scene. Time moves forward through subsequent scenes until the play is finished. Timing is everything in the theater. So it is in Director—time is the horizontal axis in the Score. Unless you stop it, a Director movie proceeds from frame to frame over time. Interactivity is based on events that occur at a certain point in time. Time is a key element in creating a Shockwave project.

Frames

The Score window is made up of **frames**. Each frame represents one instant in time. Frame 1 is at the left side of the Score, frame 2 is just to its right, and so on across the window. You can have as many frames as you need to cover the time you desire—the Score simply scrolls across to show hundreds or thousands of frames. Figure 2.4 shows these frames.

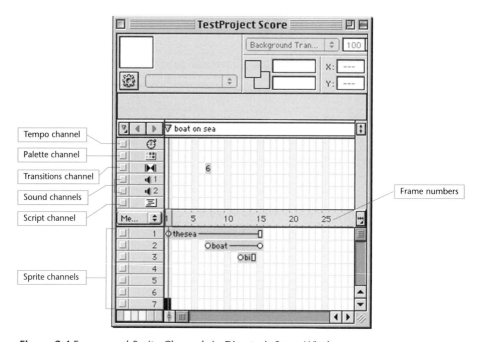

Figure 2.4 Frames and Sprite Channels in Director's Score Window

To present a continuous sequence of media elements and movements, you simply arrange the various cast members in the Score so that they appear in the proper frames. Each cast member goes into its own **sprite channel**, one of the rows down the left side of the Score, numbered from the top to the bottom. In Figure 2.4, the sea (a cast member) appears in sprite channel 1 from frame 1 to frame 15. The boat (another cast member) appears in frame 7 and stays around until frame 15. The bird appears only briefly, from frame 12 to frame 14.

In action, this movie would appear as follows. Upon opening, we see the sea. A few moments later, the boat appears sailing on the sea. Soon thereafter, the bird appears in the sky but disappears quickly. At the end, we are left with the boat on the sea, which quickly disappear as we get to frame 16. The Stage empties after frame 15, so we see nothing.

Channels

It's relatively easy to use Director to create a Shockwave movie that simply plays like a film and tells a story through the appearance and disappearance of objects, sounds, and text on the Stage over time. But to create interactivity—to let users engage with the content—you need to stop the action and give them a chance to interact. You need to stop time. And so Director includes a **script channel**, just above the frame numbers, that you can use to stop the forward movement of time, hold the action at a certain frame, and thus allow users to interact. In Chapter Five you will learn about organizing (and stopping) time in the Score and in Chapter Six how to program interactivity by the user.

Also found at the top of the Score, just above the script channel, are channels for sound, transitions, color palettes, and tempo. These are shown in Figure 2.4. These top channels are for elements and controls that are not visible on the Stage but that affect the way the movie plays. The list below describes these channels, moving from bottom to top in the window.

☆ The two **sound channels** are for the audio elements of the performance— voice, music, and sound effects. You drag audio cast members from the Cast window into these sound channels. They will not appear on the Stage because a sound has no visual representation. But when a frame with a sound in it plays, you will hear the sound.

☆ The **transitions channel** allows you to control the way the scene changes from one frame to the next—wipes, dissolves, fades, and other visual effects. You can see a transition in frame 7 of Figure 2.4, when the boat appears. Instead of simply appearing, it will dissolve in with a transition.

☆ The **color palette channel** controls how the color is rendered for certain cast members created with a nonstandard palette. Because it is seldom used in creating Shockwave movies, we will not use this channel in the book.

☆ The **tempo channel**, at the very top, is where you place instructions regarding how fast the movie plays—how quickly it proceeds from frame to frame. You can also use this channel to pause the forward motion until a certain event occurs, such as the end of a sound or a click of the mouse.

Sprite Channels

Below the frame numbers are the sprite channels. This is where the visual elements of your project go—images, videos, graphics, text, shapes, buttons, and so forth. You can have as many sprite channels as you need. Only one cast member at a time can occupy a sprite channel. In Figure 2.4, the sea, the boat, and the bird each occupy a different sprite channel. The blue bar and the name of the cast member show you what's in each channel. Notice that in the final production the boat appears in front of the sea. That's because it's in a higher sprite channel. The sea is in channel 1, which is at the back of the Stage. Channel 2 is just in front of it, so anything placed in sprite channel 2 appears in front of the item in sprite channel 1.

Movement: Sprite Position and Types

☆**WARNING** Sprite Channel Numbers versus Cast Member Numbers

Each cast member has a number based on its position in the Cast window. This is called its **member number**. When a cast member is placed on the Stage (and thus also in the Score) it is called a **sprite** and referred to by the number of the sprite channel in which it appears. So cast member 4, when placed into sprite channel 6, is called sprite 6. It's very easy for the beginning Director developer to confuse this important distinction.

Markers

Look at the bar above the channels in the Score in Figure 2.4. The small triangle with "boat on sea" next to it is called a **marker**. A marker is simply a label for a certain frame, used to show when a new scene begins. The label of this marker is "boat on sea." Another scene in this same movie, not visible in this Score, is called "sinking" and begins a scene in which the boat sinks. Markers are used to organize the various parts of your Shockwave project. When you begin to set up your own Shockwave project in Chapter Four, you will establish your own markers and assign names to them. You will also learn in Chapter Five how to use markers in scripts to control and navigate through your project.

☆**TIP**   For Flash Users

This arrangement of sprite channels is similar to the layers in Flash's Timeline except in the opposite order. In Flash, the layers nearest the top of the timeline appear in front of the layers lower down. Markers are similar to (but not exactly the same as) scenes in Flash.

The audience for your Shockwave project will never see the Score or any of these markers or channels. The Score is for you, the composer and director, to use as you create and rehearse the project. Like the concert score on the conductor's music stand, the Score window in Director lets you compose the production and then lets you watch it proceed over time as it plays. It also provides the tools for stopping the action to allow for user interactivity.

◎◎ Movement: Sprite Position and Types

The Score manages *time* in your Shockwave project; the Stage manages *space*. Each visual item in the Score has a place on the Stage. When you drag a cast member to a certain location on the Stage, it appears also in the Score. And when you drag a visual cast member into the Score, it will simultaneously appear on the Stage. Each cast member maintains a **location** on the Stage, a position that is expressed in terms of horizontal and vertical coordinates. When you build a Shockwave project, you carefully arrange all of the cast members on the Stage. When a cast member appears on the Stage, it is called a **sprite**.

Sprite Location

Some cast members, like the photo of the sea positioned in sprite channel 1 in Figure 2.4, remain in exactly the same place throughout the project. They are still called sprites, even though they do not move. Other cast members, like the boat and the bird, move across the Stage as time passes.

☆ **TIP**   **The Cartesian Plane**

Many years ago the French mathematician and philosopher René Descartes developed a system of plotting positions in space using an x-axis and a y-axis. This became the coordinate (or Cartesian) geometry you learned in high school. Any location on a flat plane (such as Director's Stage) can be defined with two numbers, one representing its position along the horizontal x-axis and the other along the vertical y-axis. This is the system used in Director to manage the location of sprites on the Stage.

Simply by dragging an item from the Cast window and dropping it on the Stage, you set its location, which Director records and remembers with a pair of numbers such as (69, 223), as shown in Figure 2.5. This indicates a spot 69 pixels across and 223 pixels down the Stage. You can see a sprite's coordinates by selecting the sprite and opening the Property Inspector window. You need not worry about these numbers—Director manages them automatically—unless you want to do some fancy sprite manipulation. You'll learn how to do this in Chapter Five.

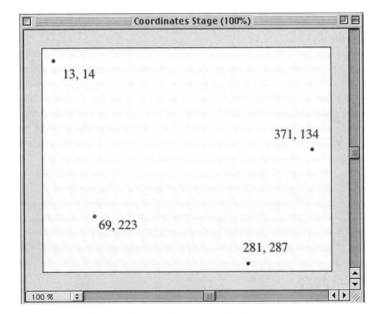

Figure 2.5 An Example of x- and y-Coordinates on the Stage

The Stage

The Stage is the centerpiece of a Shockwave project. It's where you create the action and interaction, and it's what the user sees and works with on his or her computer display. As you create your Shockwave project, you set up the Stage to look exactly as you wish. You can set its background color just as the director in a theater can paint the backdrop behind the stage. As a Shockwave developer, you can also adjust the overall size of the Stage to best fit the needs of your project and the computer display of the user. A Shockwave project can be a small item, such as a 200- by 65-pixel interactive banner ad on a Web page, or a screen-filling, television-like experience, or any size in between. The example in Figures 2.4 and 2.5 uses a Stage size of 400 by 300 pixels.

☆**TIP**   **Your Own Project**

This book will be more useful to you if you build your own Shockwave project as you proceed through the chapters. Your first project should be small in scope—an interactive advertisement or a simple game. Think of a project that will involve a dozen or so cast members, a little animation, some simple sounds, and some basic user interactivity. The example used in this book, of a boat sailing, is at about the right level for a beginning project.

As you begin to develop your own Shockwave project later in this book, you will learn to set the Stage size and background color to fit the needs of your audience and your purpose.

Kinds of Sprites

Animated Sprites

A sprite that moves across the Stage due to control by the Score or by a Lingo script as the movie proceeds from frame to frame is called an **animated sprite**. The boat in Figure 2.6 serves as an example. In frame 7 the boat is near the right edge of the Stage. In frame 8 it moves a little to the left, and in frame 9 a little more, until at frame 15 it has moved about two inches from where it started.

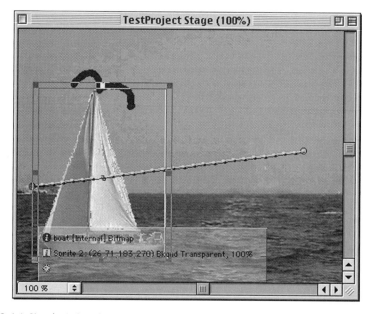

Figure 2.6 A Simple Animation

The yellow line with the dots in Figure 2.6 is the **path** for the animation. This path was created by dragging the boat across the Stage over several frames of the Score. In Chapter Five you will learn how to create path animation as well as other ways to move sprites around the Stage.

Moveable Sprites

Sprites that can be moved by the user are called **moveable sprites**. The bird in Figure 2.6 can be dragged around the sky by the user as the movie plays. The bird stays still until the user clicks and drags it. When the user lets go, the bird stops moving. This is how the interactivity of manipulation can be created. It's easy to create moveable sprites in Director and easy to program them to act in different ways.

Interactive Sprites

Some sprites respond to specific user actions—when the user rolls the pointer over them or clicks them, something happens. We call these **interactive sprites**. Anything in a Shockwave project can be made interactive. You can make the boat sink when it is clicked. You can make the bird sing as the user moves it across the Stage. You can make the bird change into an airplane when the user drags and drops it onto the island. You can make a noise or score a point when the boat sails into the island. You create this interactivity by attaching a script to a sprite. The script determines what takes place if something happens to the sprite. In Figure 2.6, the boat is in sprite channel 2 in the Score and is called sprite 2. The bird is in sprite channel 3 and is called sprite 3. This script, attached to the bird sprite, would cause the bird to sing if the user drags and drops the bird onto the boat.

```
on mouseup
    if sprite 3 intersects sprite 2 then puppetsound 1,
"birdsong"
end mouseup
```

This script tells the computer that on the event that the mouse button is released, if the bird (sprite 3) is touching the boat (sprite 2), then the cast member called "birdsong" should be played through sound channel 1. In Chapter Six you will learn how to use Lingo scripts to create many different forms of interactivity in your Shockwave projects.

The Stage with its sprites is *where* the action happens. The Score shows *when* it happens. The script determines *how* the action happens.

◎◇◎ Scripts: Behaviors and Lingo

A script tells a sprite (or some other aspect of the project) to act in a certain way. A script is like a small computer program attached to an object that controls its inter-activity. A script is like a set of specific directions given by the director to one of the actors in a play: "Hamlet, walk over to the table, face the wall, say 'To be or not to be,' then turn to the audience and say, 'That is the question.' When you see Claudius, turn away in shame." A script can be attached to a sprite, as in the exam-

Scripts: Behaviors and Lingo

ple above, or to a cast member, or to a frame, or to the entire movie. Scripts make things happen.

Scripts are written in a language called Lingo, which is built into the Director development environment. Lingo is used only in Director and reads more like a set of stage directions than like a math formula. In this way it is different from other programming languages; it's easy for novices without math backgrounds to learn. Look at the script for the interacting bird above. With a little help, you can figure it out even if you're not an experienced Lingo programmer. You will learn just enough Lingo in this book to create basic interactions in your Shockwave projects. Several good Lingo learning books are listed in the references at the end of Chapter Six. And the built-in help and scripting tools in Director will also help you compose your own scripts.

You can use scripts to navigate from one part of the project to another.

```
on mouseUp
    go to "sinking"
end mouseUp
```

This script, attached perhaps to a navigation button, tells the computer to jump to the marker labeled "sinking" in the Score.

You can use scripts to stop the forward motion of time through the Score.

```
on exitframe
    go to the frame
end exitframe
```

☆ SHORTCUT Seeing the Script

To see the script of a sprite, select the sprite, then choose Modify→Sprite→Script from the menu bar.

This script, attached to the script channel in the Score, causes the Score to stay in the frame where the script is located; every time the Score tries to exit the frame and move forward to the next frame, this script sends it back to the frame it's in. So the movie sits in an endless loop in this frame until something else happens.

You can use scripts to control sprites.

```
on exitframe
    if sprite 12 intersects sprite 14 then
        puppetsound 1, "explosion"
        set the visible of sprite 14 to false
        set thescore = thescore + 1
        go to marker(1)
    end if
    go to the frame
end exitframe
```

This more complicated script might be used in a gamelike Shockwave project. Every time the movie tries to exit the frame, it checks to see if sprites 12 and 14 have collided. If they have, the explosion sound is played through sound channel

1, sprite 14 disappears, `thescore` is incremented by one, and the movie proceeds to the next marker in the Score. If the two sprites have not collided, the movie simply loops in the same frame. A single script can cause many different actions to happen. This script also contains simple if . . . then logic, which is essential for creating responsive interactivity.

Scripts can also deal with input from the user.

```
on exitframe
    put "Who is buried in Grant's Tomb?" into field
"question1"
    if field "answer1" contains "Grant" then
        set points = points + 10
        go to "reward"
    end if
    go to the frame
end exitframe
```

This script, also in the script channel in a single frame of the project, posts a question in a text field that the user sees on the screen. Then it looks into another text field, where the user may have entered her or his answer. If what the user typed into that field contains the word "Grant," then the point score is raised by 10, and the movie goes to a frame, labeled "reward," in which the user is congratulated for a correct answer. If the answer field contains something other than "Grant," or nothing at all, the movie loops again through the frame it is in.

Scripts give directions, test to see whether certain conditions have occurred, and make things happen. Scripts consist of handlers (`on  mouseUp`), commands (`go to . . .`), logic (`if . . . then . . . else`), and comparisons (`field "answer1" contains "Grant"`). Scripts can be attached to sprites, to cast members, to frames, or to the entire movie. In Chapter Six you will learn to use these scripts to create simple interactions. You will also learn to use Director's **built-in behaviors**, which are scripts included with Director that help you create common animations and interactions.

◎◎ Creating a Simple Production

The best way to get to know the Shockwave development environment is to create a small project and watch it work. This little test project is just for this chapter; you will not follow it throughout the book. It's simply a way to get your hands on the software and get a feel for how it works, in advance of building your own project as you work through subsequent chapters.

Go to a computer with the latest version of Director installed, and follow the directions below. This test project uses files you can download by going to the Web Wizard Web site at `http://www.aw.com/info/webwizard/` and then following the path to the Teaching Resources for this book. The files are called `Chapter 2 Test Project`. You are going to build the boat project you saw earlier in this chapter.

1. Download the files.

    a. Download the files at the Web Wizard Web site to the desktop of your computer.

    b. Decompress (unzip or unstuff) them as necessary until you see three files:

        ★ `thesea.jpg`

        ★ `boat.jpg`

        ★ `birdsong.aif`

2. Import the elements.

    a. Open Director.

    b. Open the windows for the Stage, the Cast, and the Score. Also open the Control Panel.

    c. From the File menu, choose Import, and import the three files you just downloaded to your desktop. Watch them appear in the Cast window. Your Cast window should look something like Figure 2.7.

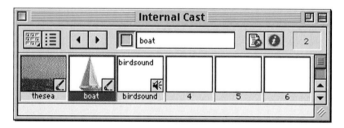

Figure 2.7 The Cast Window for the Test Project

☆**TIP**   **Cast Window Appearance**

Director's Cast window can be arranged in two different ways: as a list of filenames or as an array of thumbnails. In this book, we use the thumbnail arrangement, which makes it easier to see the nature of each cast member at a glance. To change the way the Cast window looks, click the Cast View Style button at the top left of the Cast window. It's the little button that looks like the icon shown here.

---

3. Drag the sea to the Stage.

    a. Drag the thumbnail of the sea from the Cast window and drop it on the Stage, in the center. The sea thumbnail will appear on the Stage, and you'll see it fill sprite channel 1 in the Score.

4. Drag the boat to the Stage.

    a. Drag the thumbnail of the boat from the Cast window to the Stage. Drop it on the sea. You will see it appear on the Stage, on top of the sea. You will also see it appear in sprite channel 2 of the Score.

5. *Make the boat's background transparent.*

   a. Open the Property Inspector window by choosing Inspectors→Property from the Window menu. You will see a window that looks like Figure 2.8, containing everything you ever wanted to know about this boat.

   b. From the pop-up menu next to the inkwell, choose Background Transparent. This makes the white background around the boat transparent.

   c. Close the Property Inspector window.

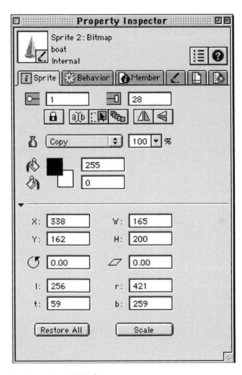

Figure 2.8 The Property Inspector Window

6. *Animate the boat.*

   a. Select the boat on the Stage.

   b. Drag its registration point—the little red and green dot in the center—across the Stage along the path you want the boat to follow. The path will appear as a yellow line with dots along it. Your Stage should look something like Figure 2.9.

7. *Play the movie.*

   a. Click the rewind button in the Control Panel. Watch the playhead in the Score move back to frame 1.

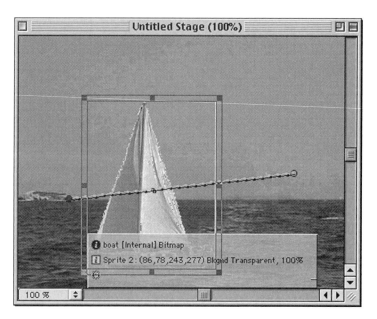

Figure 2.9 The Stage with the Animated Boat

    b. Click the play button in the Control Panel. The boat will sail across the sea.

    c. Click the stop button in the Control panel, then rewind to frame 1.

8. Save your work.

    a. Choose Save from the File menu.

    b. Give your project the name `TestProject.dir`, and save it in the same folder as its media elements. The `.dir` file extension tells the computer that this is a Director file. This file contains all your work—the Score, the Scripts, the images, the sound, the Stage—in a special format that can be opened and edited only in Director.

9. Draw the bird.

    a. In the Cast window, select cast member 4, which should be empty.

    b. Choose Paint from the Window menu. In this Paint window you will draw a simple little bird to place in the sky.

    c. Select a dark blue color from the Foreground Color chip. Then select the paintbrush tool. Draw a bird, as shown in Figure 2.10. You will see the bird's thumbnail in the Cast window.

10. Drag the bird to the Stage.

    a. Drag the bird from the Cast window into the sky on the Stage.

    b. Make its background transparent using the Property Inspector window, as you did with the boat in step 5.

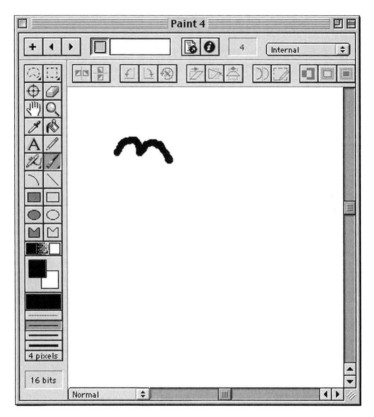

Figure 2.10 Drawing a Bird in the Paint Window

11. *Make the bird sing.*

a. Select the bird.

b. Open the Behavior Inspector window—you'll find it under Inspectors in the Window menu.

c. From the behavior pop-up (the + sign) choose New Behavior. Name this behavior `sing`.

d. From the event pop-up (also a +) choose MouseUp. (A MouseUp event happens when the user clicks the mouse. A click has two parts: a MouseDown and a MouseUp.)

e. From the action pop-up (+) choose Sound→Play Cast Member. Specify `birdsound` as the cast member you want to play. Click OK. Your Behavior Inspector window should look like Figure 2.11. The bird now has a script attached to it that will cause the bird sound to play whenever the bird is clicked.

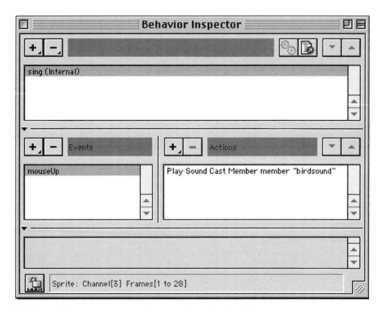

Figure 2.11 The Behavior Inspector Window for the Bird Script

12. Test your movie.

a. Rewind to the beginning and play the movie. The boat will animate.

b. Click the bird to hear it sing. If it doesn't work as it's supposed to, go back through these instructions and check your work. Also check your work against Figure 2.12.

13. Save your project as a Shockwave file.

a. So far, you have been working in Director, authoring this sample project. You see all the windows and have complete control over the process. Now it's time to see the project as the audience will see it on the Web, which is very different from how it looks to you.

b. Choose Publish. . . from the File menu. Director will compress your project and save the necessary parts in the Shockwave format, with the filename extension `.dcr`. It will also create a Web page for you, in which the Shockwave file is embedded. The process of publishing will also automatically open this Web page in your browser.

14. Test your Shockwave project in a Web browser.

a. As soon as the file is loaded, you will see the boat move across the screen. When you click on the bird, it will sing.

Congratulations on developing your first Shockwave project! If you look in your project folder, you will see two new files, `TestProject.dcr` (the Shockwave file) and `TestProject.html` (the Web page in which the project is embedded).

Figure 2.12 The Test Project Windows

You have just experienced the process, from beginning to end, of developing a simple Shockwave project. From importing the elements to testing the final project in a browser, you have witnessed and participated in all the steps. As you continue working through this book, you will go through this process step-by-step, adding details and getting guidance as you produce more complex projects. Consider yourself newly apprenticed to a digital playwright, who also does casting and directing. So far, you've only put a few actors on the stage and let them carry on a brief drama with little movement and minimal interaction. But you'll soon go on to design, write, prepare, arrange, and rehearse a more complex piece, one that will debut on the Web as a Shockwave project.

☆ **WARNING** The Shockwave Plug-in

You will not be able to see your test project in the browser unless you have the current version of the Shockwave Player installed. If you experience a plug-in error, connect to `http://sdc.shockwave.com/shockwave/download/`, where you can download the plug-in. Follow the installation instructions carefully.

☆ Summary

▷ Shockwave developers works mostly with the Stage, Score, and Cast windows of Macromedia Director. The Stage is *where* the action occurs, the Score shows *when* it happens, and the Cast comprises *who* does the acting. Scripts direct *how* it happens.

▷ A cast member when on the Stage is called a *sprite*.

▷ Whenever they are on the Stage, sprites show in the *frames* of the Score. The frames can be grouped into scenes with *markers*.

▷ Animation occurs when a sprite changes its position on the Stage over time, usually through a string of frames. Location on the Stage is measured in pixels on a coordinate plane.

▷ *Scripts* are written in Director's Lingo scripting language. Scripts direct the action of sprites, cast members, frames, and other aspects of a Shockwave project.

▷ Creating a Shockwave project begins with the preparation of its various media elements, which are imported into Director, arranged on the Stage and in the Score, animated, and scripted. The completed project is saved in the Shockwave format and displayed in a Web page.

☆ Online References

Answers to common questions about Director, from Macromedia
`http://www.macromedia.com/support/director/ts/documents/presalesfaq.htm`

Tips on how to manage a multimedia production in Director
`http://www.macromedia.com/support/director/how/expert/manage/`

An animated tutorial on cast members and sprites
`http://www.macromedia.com/support/director/how/show/castmembers.html`

The Director Online User Group
`http://www.director-online.com/`

Sample files for the test project in this chapter
`http://www.aw.com/webwizard/`

⭐ Review Questions

1. Name the four main windows and palettes in the Shockwave programming environment and explain the function of each.

2. Explain the theater metaphor for development in Director and what each of the main windows represents.

3. List the kinds of media files Director can import and the programs you can use to prepare each kind.

4. Explain the difference between frames and sprite channels in the Score window.

5. Trace the process of animating a sprite in the Score with path animation.

6. What are moveable sprites, and why might they be used in a Shockwave project?

7. Why do you need scripts, and how are they written?

8. Describe the steps in creating a simple Shockwave project.

⭐ Hands-On Exercises

1. Open Director. Open the four main windows (Stage, Score, Cast, Control Panel). Also open the Tool Palette. Close all other windows. Arrange the windows as shown in Figure 2.1. Set the Stage size to 400 by 300 pixels.

2. Prepare three media elements, using the programs described in this chapter:

   ⭐ A large background image, 400 by 300 pixels in size

   ⭐ A small foreground image, about 100 by 100 pixels

   ⭐ A small sound file, saved in `.aif` format

   Save them all in a single folder on your hard disk. Import these files into Director.

3. Place the first two cast members from exercise 2 onto the Stage, and place the other in the sound channel of the Score. Animate the foreground image using simple path animation.

4. Develop the test project described at the end of this chapter. Download the files from the Web Wizard Web site, import them, animate the boat, and make the bird sing.

5. Save the test project as a Shockwave file, and test it in a Web browser.

CHAPTER THREE

PLANNING AND PREPARING

Therefore prepare thee to cut off the flesh.
Shed thou no blood; nor cut thou less, nor more,
But just a pound of flesh.

—from *The Merchant of Venice*

Director provides the skeleton of your Shockwave project—the stage, the score, empty seats for the cast, and a language to write scripts. But *you* must put the flesh on the bones, first by planning the production, then by creating the media elements. In this chapter you'll learn how to plan your project, set a schedule, and prepare the pieces—the pounds of flesh—that will bring the project to life. As you prepare these pieces, you'll learn to trim them to the optimal proportions for use on the Web.

Chapter Objectives

☆ To learn a process for planning and scheduling a Shockwave project

☆ To learn how to set up Director for the project you have planned

⭐ To learn how to prepare elements generally created in other programs (for example, text, images, sound, video) and how to use Director's tools to prepare other elements (for example, shapes, vector graphics, unedited sound)

Planning the Shockwave Project

Beginning here in Chapter Three and continuing through Chapter Eight, you will build your own Shockwave project. The best way to learn Shockwave is to use it, and the best way to build a project is to begin with a carefully thought-out plan. A project development *plan*, a *schedule* of steps to track your progress, and a *flow chart* are essential to a successful project.

Writing a Project Development Plan

Every Shockwave project on the Web serves a purpose, aims at a particular audience, and possesses a unique structure and features. Before you begin working on your own project, you need a plan that sets forth these essential concepts. In the professional world of Web development, no project is begun or funded without such a plan, approved in advance. The elements of a Shockwave project plan are described briefly below.

Executive Summary

This leadoff item is a summary of the project development plan, the essence of the project described in three or four sentences. Normally written *after* the entire plan is complete, it should summarize most of the other elements of the plan.

Statement of Purpose

Here you set forth the ideas that you expect the Shockwave project to communicate, the context in which it will be used, and the reasons this project is necessary. You describe the problem to be solved, and you summarize how you expect the audience to act or think differently after using this project.

Definition of Audience

In this section you describe the people you expect to use this project, along with how and why they will use it. You provide some background on how this audience perceives the topics and ideas that are the substance of your project. You also describe where and when the audience is likely to use the project.

System Requirements

In this technical part you describe the equipment and software with which this Shockwave project will run. You should be quite specific about the hardware and software systems, including the operating systems, processor speed, display size, browser, and plug-ins necessary to make it work. Also include information on the availability of those systems among the intended audience.

Competition

Here you consider and describe the alternate ways of communicating your ideas to the intended audience, including traditional and less expensive methods. You may also describe any interactive examples currently available on the Web that communicate a similar message. You should describe the shortcomings of these alternatives and explain why your new Shockwave project is necessary.

Structure

You set forth the overall structure of the product, including how the information is organized and how the user encounters and interacts with it. You should list the sections or parts of the product and describe the content of each section. You should also describe the nature of the materials to be used (text, image, video, sound, animation) and the projected source of each. Finally, explain any permissions issues that might affect publishing your Shockwave project.

Methods, Features, and Design

In this part you explain how you will present information and how the user will interact with the program. You should also list any important or unique features of your project, as well as its basic design elements and approaches. Finally, you should explain how the user will navigate through the product.

Development Environment

Describe the software tools you will use to prepare the elements and assemble the work, and specify how you will deliver the Shockwave project to the user. Explain why you chose Shockwave, and compare it with alternative development tools you might have used. Describe the skills needed by the developers of this project.

User Walk-through

Describe "a minute in the life" of a typical user working with your Shockwave project. In some detail, spell out exactly what the user does and thinks when using your project and why the user makes choices and responds as she or he does.

Budget

Estimate the expenditures necessary to produce this project. Include expenses for:

☆ *Personnel*: payments to the people who will prepare the materials, program in Director, test the project, and manage the process

☆ *Permissions and royalties*: payments to copyright holders of materials you might use

☆ *Source material*: the cost of acquiring or creating text, video, images, photos, drawings, music, sound, and other media elements

☆ *Equipment*: the cost of purchasing or renting computers, cameras, scanners, and other equipment

Personnel

A large Shockwave project may need a team of developers—a designer, an animator, a Lingo scripter, a text editor, quality testers, and others who contribute their skills to a combined entity managed by a project manager. Describe the personnel needed to create the project.

You should *write* this project development plan because the act of writing helps you think through the details in advance. You should also share it with other persons involved in the project, most importantly your client, your supervisor, and perhaps even members of the target audience. After revising the plan based on their feedback, keep it handy because you'll need it later as you begin to build the project.

Setting a Project Schedule

Designing and building a Shockwave production is a multistep process that's best done in a certain order. Just as the playwright must compose the script before the director hires the actors, and the set designer must paint the scenery before the audience arrives, you must build your project in a certain order. A project schedule spells out the order of events in building a Shockwave project and lists an estimated date for each milestone. These events are shown in Table 3.1, which you can use to schedule your own project. A blank copy of this table is included on the Web Wizard Web site, in the Teacher Support section for this book.

Table 3.1 Steps in the Shockwave Development Schedule

Event	Date
1. *A great idea.* No product succeeds unless it is founded on a clear and important idea. Think up a great idea for the product, talk it over with people, and work out the details in your mind.	
2. *Product development plan.* This is the plan described in the text. Finish creating the plan before you take the following steps.	
3. *Paper prototype.* Choose a chunk of your product—one complete section, perhaps—and spell it out on paper. Include a written description of what a user would do. Include sketches of how the screens will look. Show this prototype to the client, the users, and your coworkers. Revise as necessary.	
4. *Static prototype.* Take what you set forth with the paper prototype and develop it on the computer screen with Director. At this point, just develop what the user will see at various steps in the interaction; there's no need yet to make it operational. Show this static prototype to the client, the users, and your coworkers. Make changes as necessary.	

Table 3.1 *(continued)*

Event	Date
5. *Operational prototype.* Add logic and interaction to your static prototype. Make all the buttons work and the fields live. Make it work exactly as the final product will work. Test this operational prototype with the kinds of people you expect will use the final product, on the kinds of computers you expect they'll use. Show it also to the client and your coworkers. Revise from what you learn.	
6. *Production.* Gather and edit the raw materials for the rest of the project, assemble them on the computer, and program the interaction, section by section. Test the project yourself as you go along to make sure it is working. Test pieces of it with users, on the target equipment.	
7. *Alpha testing.* Save the project in Shockwave format, and embed it in a Web page. Provide it, along with instructions, to a small group of users. As they use it on the target platform, gather their feedback about reactions and problems. Revise the project as necessary.	
8. *Beta testing.* Provide your product, in the form in which it will be published, to a set of typical users, and watch what they do. Make sure they use the project on their own computers, so you can test compatibility and plug-in procedures. Try to include several different types of people, computers, and browsers among your beta testers. Careful observation of these beta testers will help you find yet more ways to improve your work.	
9. *Shipping.* Publish your many-times-revised Shockwave project on the Web. Provide it to users. Enjoy the accolades for work well done.	
10. *Develop version 2.0.* Collect feedback from users of your product. Design new features, add content, and otherwise make the product stronger, deeper, and better. Go back to step 6 and repeat the process.	

As you use this book to develop your Shockwave project, you can use Table 3.1 to record your progress.

Drawing a Flow Chart

Most Shockwave projects, because they are interactive, include more than one scene, event, or possibility. There is most often a sequence of events, a collection of separate scenes, an array of choices, or a set of possible actions. Each of these parts of your project should be shown on a flow chart. This chart is a diagram of your product that uses boxes and arrows to illustrate the structure and depth of the material and to show user options and paths. In this book, we use the flow chart as a dynamic planning and development tool.

Look back at your project plan, and review the sections on structure, methods, and the user walk-through. This will help you think through the items that should appear on the flow chart.

In the flow chart, draw a rectangle for each scene or section of your project. Connect the rectangles to show the paths the user can take through the scenes (or the choices and reactions to various events). You can draw your flow chart on paper or create it with text boxes and arrows in Microsoft Word. As you organize and prepare materials for your project, you will use your flow chart for annotations and record keeping, so make sure it's available to you later. Figure 3.1 shows a flow chart for a typical Shockwave project.

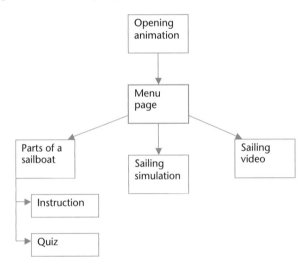

Figure 3.1 Flow Chart for Shockwave Project

☆ **SHORTCUT** **Flow Charts with Microsoft Word**

To create a simple flow chart quickly, open a Word document, choose Insert→Text box from the menu bar, then click and drag a rectangle about 2 inches square. Type the name of a project section into the textbox. Repeat this process to create boxes for the other sections of the project. Drag them around the page to arrange them, then use Word's line tool to connect the boxes to show the links between sections.

◎◎ Organizing and Labeling the Production

Before preparing the pieces of your project, it's a good idea to set it up in Director and make some decisions about how it will look. This will make your preparations more efficient and provide a solid environment in which to import the elements.

Setting the Stage Size

How big will your Shockwave project be? Will it advertise a product on a Web site, to fit within a standard 468 by 60-pixel spot? Or will it be a screen-filling experience that takes over the entire browser window? A Shockwave project has a fixed size, which you must determine at the outset.

Many factors will influence your decision about the size of the Stage, including those listed below.

 The display size of your target audience's computers. While most Web users see pages on a computer display 800 pixels wide and 600 pixels high, not all do. A few are restricted to 640 by 480 pixel displays, while others enjoy 1,024 by 768 pixel and larger displays. Most Shockwave developers design for the 800 by 600-pixel display, but this does not mean that the Stage size of your Shockwave project should be set to 800 by 600 pixels. In most cases, the audience will see your Shockwave project in a Web browser window. The title bars, toolbars, address bar, status bar, and scrollbars of this browser window take up so much space that the viewable area of the browser for most users ends up at about 760 by 420 pixels. So if your Shockwave project is going to be embedded in a Web page, the maximum Stage size you can consider is 760 by 420 pixels. But the maximum Stage size is not always the best choice.

 The bandwidth enjoyed by your target audience. A big Stage needs big scenery to fill it. For projects with lots of bitmapped (photographic) images, a Stage-filling background can demand many kilobytes of data. The more data in your project, the longer it takes the viewer to receive it. So if your audience typically uses a telephone modem to access the Web, you must keep the file size of your Shockwave project as small as possible. Even with the compression that Shockwave provides, a typical 760 by 420-pixel photo can take up about 75KB of data, which might take 15 seconds to arrive. Five such photos in a Shockwave project could keep users waiting for more than a minute. Reducing the Stage size, and thus the size of the photos, to 400 by 300 pixels would cut the size of the Shockwave file, and the length of the download time, about in half.

 The nature of the material you are presenting. How much room do you really need to get your point across and allow for user interactivity? How many choices need to be visible at once? How big are the objects that the user will manipulate? How many cast members need to be visible at once? How much text do you need to fit on the screen at any one time? How many pixels do you need to show the detail in the photo? The answers to these kinds of questions will help you determine the optimal Stage size for your project.

 The context in which your Shockwave project will appear. Will your project be embedded in a Web page with other text or image material? How much room will be left for the Shockwave project? Or will it open in its own window? What else might the typical user need to see on her or his display while interacting with the Shockwave project? You need to consider this as well before settling on the best Stage size. It's not wise to change Stage size later in the process, so it's best to think through these considerations in the setup phase.

To set the Stage size, choose Modify→Movie→Properties from the Director's menu bar. This opens the Property Inspector window for the movie, in which you can enter the height and width of the Stage in pixels (Figure 3.2).

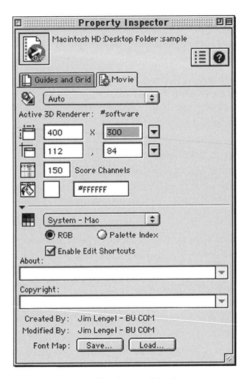

Figure 3.2 Setting the Stage Size for a Shockwave Movie

☆**WARNING Too Big!**

If you set the Stage size of your project too large, you will prevent users from seeing the entire screen. You'll also increase the file size of your project because every image will need to be bigger in order to fill the larger Stage. Big files mean long download times. So pay attention to the display size—within the browser window—of your target audience.

Creating Markers in the Score

Most Shockwave projects consist of several distinct parts or scenes. You should set up each of these scenes in the Score with markers as part of the setup process. As explained in Chapter Two, a marker denotes the frame at which the scene or section begins. For the project shown in the flow chart in Figure 3.1, the markers in the Score might look like those shown in Figure 3.3.

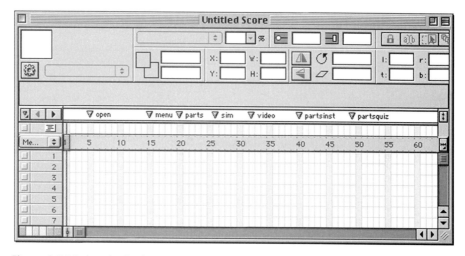

Figure 3.3 Markers in the Score

Later, when you assemble the elements of your Shockwave project, you will place the elements into the appropriate place in the Score as denoted by these markers. To create a marker, simply click in the marker area at the top of the Score window. Then enter from the keyboard a name for the marker. For ease of reference later, keep the names of your markers brief, as in the example in Figure 3.3.

☆**TIP**   **Marker Labels**

The names for your markers are more than signposts on the Score. They are the words that will denote the various sections of your project. You will use these marker names repeatedly in your scripting, so be sure to make the labels meaningful and short, a single word if possible. And don't use the same label more than once.

Don't worry, you can add and delete markers later, and you can also easily adjust the number of frames between the markers. To remove a marker, simply drag it up out of the marker area. Markers organize your project in the Score window, so it's good to set them up at the outset.

Listing the Media Elements

Refer back to your flow chart, and choose one rectangle for further analysis. In order to build this part of the project, what media elements will you need? Make a list. Consider all the media: text, images, voice, music, animation, and video. If we were to list the media elements for the project in the flow chart in Figure 3.1, for the section that identifies the parts of the boat, our list might look like Table 3.2.

Table 3.2 Media Elements for the Boat Project

Media	Element(s)
Text	Labels for each part of the boat
	Instructions
Images	The sea background
	The boat
	Parts of the boat: jib, mainsail, rudder, tiller, mast, keel
Sound	Voice describing each part: jib, mainsail, rudder, tiller, mast, keel
	Hornpipe background music
Video	Boat sailing
Animation	Tiller and rudder moving in tandem

A list like this is created for each part of the project, for each rectangle in the flow chart. Even a small Shockwave project requires a substantial collection of elements. The list you create at this step in the process will guide you in the next task: the preparation of the individual media elements.

◎◎ Preparing the Media Elements

For some Shockwave projects, the preparation of each of the many media elements makes up the bulk of the creative work. This is an essential step that must be accomplished carefully and well so that subsequent steps of assembly can proceed smoothly and the finished project can reflect high quality. Preparing the elements is like hiring the actors and making sure they know their lines before putting them on the stage.

Shockwave provides only minimal tools for the preparation of the elements, so this step requires the use of other multimedia software tools such as Photoshop and SoundEdit. From the list of elements you created during the last step, prepare each in turn.

☆ **TIP   Chunking and Prototyping**

You need not prepare *all* the media elements for *all* sections of your Shockwave project before doing any assembly in Director. It's better to choose one chunk or section of your project and build it through to completion by preparing all its elements, assembling them in Director, programming the interactivity, and publishing the result to a Web browser. It's similar to memorizing and rehearsing one scene of the play to work out all the glitches before tackling the entire production. The experience you gain by building a small chunk as a prototype will enable you to produce subsequent sections more efficiently.

Preparing Text

Director provides excellent text-formatting tools but doesn't have a spelling checker. So it's a good idea to compose the text passages for your project in a word processor and to check the spelling and grammar there. From the word processor, save the text as a Rich Text Format (`.rtf`) file, which will preserve most of the formatting when you import the text into Director.

☆ **WARNING** Filename Extensions

The dot and the three letters that end the filename are important aspects of your work. The computer needs those filename extensions to help determine what kind of file it is. As you prepare the individual media files for your Shockwave project, make sure you save each one with the filename extension that matches its file format.

Preparing Images

In most cases, you should use an image-editing program such as Photoshop to get your bitmap images ready for importing into Director. Photoshop has many tools and techniques you can use to make your images just right.

Image Size

Decide in advance exactly how big your image will be when it shows up in Director. Director works much better and much faster if it doesn't have to shrink or stretch images as it plays. So if you want an image to cover one-fourth of the screen in your project, then use Photoshop to change the image size to about 400 by 300 pixels. Since the display area of most computer monitors is 800 by 600 pixels, you can be sure that the 400 by 300 image will exactly fill one-quarter of the screen. Photoshop does a better job at resizing images than Director does. To change the size of an image in Photoshop, use the Image Size... command under the Image menu.

Image Depth

This is a measure of how much color information your image contains. The greater the color depth, the more realistic the picture. Color depth can range from 1 bit (black and white) to 32 bits (millions of colors). In a 1-bit image, each pixel can be either black or white. In a 32-bit image, each pixel is represented by 32 numbers and so can take on millions of different colors. As you might expect, 32-bit images take up 32 times more room on the disk—and 32 times more space in memory—than 1-bit images. They also take 32 times longer to travel over the Internet. There is a price to pay for such good color. The price is paid not only in disk space, but also in speed: it will take Director considerably longer to display a 32-bit image than a 16-bit or 8-bit image. If you want your color images to come up very quickly, use 8-bit color. If you want your pictures to look good and are willing to wait a bit for them, use 16-bit color. But remember that most computers display 16-bit color. So if you intend to publish your work to run on mainstream computers on the World Wide Web, use nothing more than 16-bit color throughout. You can change the color depth in Photoshop by using the Index Color command from the Mode menu. In most cases, you should select 16-bit color, using the System palette.

☆WARNING Anti-aliasing

In a word: don't. Many image-editing programs are set up to *anti-alias* the objects that you draw or paste into them. This is an adjustment to the image that makes it appear smoothly against the background, avoiding the jagged edges caused by the square corners of the pixels. Anti-aliasing inserts extra pixels at the edges whose color is halfway between the color of the object and the color of the background. So a black object on a white background would end up with extra gray pixels all around the edge. The problem arises when this same object is placed against a different color background. The extra pixels at the edges form a sort of halo around the object. So shut off anti-aliasing in your image-editing program as you prepare elements for your Shockwave project.

Image Format

Save your images in JPEG or PNG format, which Director can handle best. If you have an image in some other file format, such as PICT, BMP, or TIFF, you can open it with Photoshop and then save it as a JPEG or PNG file. When you save the file, use a filename in the form of `picture.jpg` or `picture.png`, respectively. This will ensure its operability on both Macintosh and Windows computers.

Image Compression

Compressed images take less space on the disk, and they travel faster over the Web. But they lose some quality. When you choose Save for Web… from Photoshop's File menu, you will be able to choose the amount of compression you desire and see the effect on image quality. *The Web Wizard's Guide to Multimedia* provides more detailed information on the how and why of image compression.

Image Style

Make sure your images are crisp and clear with no rough spots or ragged edges. Use Photoshop as necessary to crop, sharpen, lighten, or clean up your images. Be especially on the lookout for black or white around the edges. Avoid using Photoshop to add text to your images. It's better to save your images without labels or words; you can add text over the images in Director, where you will have better control of the appearance and interactivity of the text.

☆WARNING Only for Bitmaps

This section on preparing images applies only to bitmap images, the kind that are defined pixel by pixel and edited in Photoshop, mostly photographic images. Vector graphic images, such as those drawn in Adobe Illustrator or Macromedia Freehand, are prepared differently, as described later in this chapter.

Preparing Edited Sound

Sounds are used in Shockwave in two different ways:

1. *As sound cast members placed in the sound channel of the Score.* This is the "normal" way to bring sound into Shockwave. You should use SoundEdit or

SoundForge to prepare the sound and then save the sound in a format you can import into Director. The filenames should end with the suffix `.aif`, such as `soundname.aif`, or as Shockwave audio with the `.swf` extension.

2. *As QuickTime video cast members placed in a regular sprite channel.* Use this method if you want to use the timing of the sound to synchronize the animations on the screen. Save the sound as a QuickTime movie to use this method. These files should be named in the format `soundname.mov`.

No matter which method you choose, the sounds should share the characteristics listed below.

Sampling Rate

When you digitize a sound, the computer samples the sound many times each second. The more frequent the sampling, and the more data in each sample, the better it sounds. The highest rate at which your computer can sample is 44,000 times per second, 16 bits per sample. This is the same rate used by music CDs and is better than most human ears can hear. But such sounds take up enormous disk space and take a long time to download over the Web. So when you capture sound, use this highest rate. Then edit the sound until you have exactly what you need. When it comes time to save your sound, save two copies: one at the high sampling rate and another that's compressed. You'll learn more about compression below.

Mono or Stereo

Stereo sound takes up twice the disk space and download time of mono. It also sounds better. If music is central to your project, if users will have stereo speakers connected to their computers, and if the stereo effect is essential, then save your files in stereo. Otherwise, use SoundEdit to mix the sound to mono before saving.

File Format

Director can import sounds from a variety of formats: AIFF (Audio Interchange File Format), WAV, MP3, MOV (QuickTime), and SWA (Shockwave Audio). So you need to save your sounds in one of these formats. You can place all of these formats in the sound channel of the Score except for QuickTime (`.mov`) files, which go into a sprite channel. Do not save your sounds in SoundEdit format, which Director and other programs cannot read. Use the naming conventions shown in Table 3.3 as you save your sound files.

Compression

Since a Shockwave project is in most cases delivered over the Web, it is essential that you compress sound elements to be as small as possible in file size before they are imported into Director. All of the audio file formats listed in Table 3.3 except WAV can compress the data as the file is saved. Compression lowers sound quality to some degree, but if you do it well, this reduction is not evident to the listener. To show the results of compression, we recorded a 6-second narration of the type that might be used in a Shockwave project. (The raw sound data was sampled at 44kHz, 16-bit mono.) We then saved it in several different formats and compression ratios. Table 3.4 shows the results.

Table 3.3 Sound File Formats for Shockwave Projects

File Format	Filename Extension	Program to Use
Audio Interchange File Format	`.aif`	SoundEdit, SoundForge, QuickTime Player Pro
Waveform	`.wav`	Windows Sound Recorder, SoundForge, QuickTime Player Pro
QuickTime	`.mov`	SoundEdit, QuickTime Player Pro
Shockwave Audio	`.swa`	SoundEdit
Moving Picture Experts Group	`.mp3`	MP3PRO, iTunes

Table 3.4 Comparison of File Sizes with Various Audio Formats

File Format	File Size, Uncompressed	File Size, Compressed	Filename Extension	Comments
Audio Interchange File Format	552 K	32K	`.aif`	
Moving Picture Experts Group	—	68K	`.mp3`	Compressed format only
QuickTime	552K	36K	`.mov`	
Shockwave Audio	—	28K	`.swa`	Compressed format only
Waveform	544K	—	`.wav`	No compression possible

Preparing the Media Elements

☆TIP   Codecs

To compress audio and video files for Shockwave, the sound-preparation software uses a **codec**, short for compressor-decompressor, which is special computer code that removes data unnecessary to the listener. The Shockwave developer compresses the file, imports the compressed file into Director, and publishes it on the Web. The listener's computer decompresses the audio file and plays it through the speakers. You can learn more about audio compression from *The Web Wizard's Guide to Multimedia*.

To prepare a sound file for use in Shockwave, you must first capture the sound from its source; then edit it as necessary with sound-editing software; and finally save and compress it in one of the file formats that Director can import.

☆**TIP**   **Sample Music Files**

To help you practice with audio in Shockwave, you can download some sample music files from the Web Wizard Web site. The composers' copyrights on these samples have long since expired, so you have permission to use these samples in your Shockwave project and to publish them on the Web.

Preparing Unedited Sound

Short sounds that will need no editing can be recorded directly into your Shockwave project, but only in the Macintosh version of Director. Choose Insert→Media Element→Sound... from Director's menu bar. You will see a recording panel with record, stop, and play buttons, similar to what you see in Figure 3.4. To record a sound, click the record button, make the sound, then click the stop button. Click the play button to hear the sound. If it is acceptable, save the sound, and it will appear in the Cast window. This sound can be used in the Score and called from Lingo scripts as can any other sound in your project.

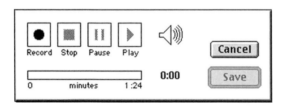

Figure 3.4 Sound Recording Panel

Preparing Video

You can use video in a Shockwave project, but beware that video files are large in size, slow to download, and may not perform well for audiences on a telephone modem connection. But if the target audience for your Web site enjoys a LAN, cable modem, or DSL connection with good bandwidth (400 kilobits per second or better), then video can work well if properly prepared.

The best results occur with videos at 12 or 15 frames per second, no bigger than 320 by 240 pixels, compressed using the latest codecs such as Sorenson Video. Shockwave can deal with both downloaded and streaming video. Video for Shockwave should be saved in either the QuickTime (.mov) or Video for Windows

Preparing the Media Elements

(.avi) format. Most Shockwave projects use QuickTime video clips because Director provides an array of tools for this form of video, so the instructions in this book are based on the .mov format. (For more information on video formats and streaming, consult *The Web Wizard's Guide to Multimedia*. That book also provides a more detailed guide to capturing, editing, and saving video.)

Capture Video

Video for a Shockwave project can come from a variety of sources, for example, an existing videotape, live video shot with a camcorder, or existing digital video files. If the video files have already been captured digitally, you can skip this step. For the two analog sources, you need a computer with video-capture and -editing software, along with a VCR or camcorder. The most commonly used systems for preparing video for Shockwave projects are shown in Table 3.5.

Table 3.5 Video-Editing Software

Software	Platform	Comments
iMovie	Macintosh only	Easiest to use, least expensive
Premiere	Macintosh or Windows	Older technology, expensive
Final Cut Pro	Macintosh only	Most expensive

No matter which system you use, the process is the same.

1. Connect the video camcorder or VCR to the computer.

2. Launch the video-editing software.

3. Import the video and audio from the VCR or camcorder to the computer.

4. Assemble the video clips in the timeline.

5. Edit the video, trimming and adding narration, titles, and special effects.

6. Save and compress the video in a form suitable for Shockwave.

☆ **TIP**   **Shooting Good Video**

Shooting video for a Shockwave project is not like shooting a home movie or a TV show. Because the video will be smaller than the full screen size, you need to make sure your subject fills the screen—use close shots. Pay attention to the lighting. Because the file will be compressed and will play at low frame rates, you should avoid rapid pans, zooms, or complex backgrounds. And don't forget the audio—always use an external microphone to capture your subject's speech.

Edit Video

Video for Shockwave is more effective when it's tightly edited and kept brief. Edit down to only what you absolutely need. Avoid looping logos and other special effects that do not translate well to Web video. Make sure the audio track is clear and strong. If you must use titles, make them large enough to be legible at the reduced size of the video window. Keep it simple, and keep it short.

Save and Compress Video

The video must be saved (or exported, depending on which editing software you use) in a format that Director can work with. The most flexible format is QuickTime, with the `.mov` file extension. All the common video-editing systems can export to QuickTime. As you save or export, you will have the opportunity to set the specifications of the video. These are critical to good performance, so take this step carefully.

☆ *Size.* Keep the video no larger than 320 by 240 pixels. This is the largest than can be safely transmitted to most Web users today.

☆ *Frame rate.* Do not exceed 15 frames per second. For most video, 12 frames per second is adequate. Increasing the frame rate calls for much more data to be sent over the Web and will not significantly improve performance.

☆ *Video compression.* Use a common codec such as Sorenson Video or Cinepak. Your editing software will let you make this choice as you save the video, as shown in Figure 3.5.

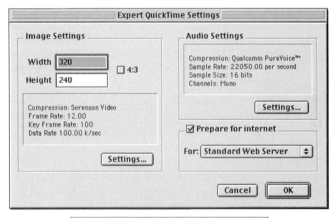

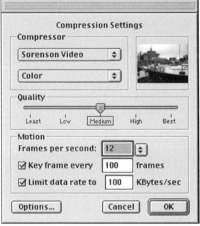

Figure 3.5 Choosing the Video Compression Codec

The video shown in Figure 3.5 is being saved in the QuickTime format, 320 by 240 pixels in size, at 12 frames per second, using the Sorenson Video codec and the Qualcomm PureVoice audio codec.

> ### ☆ SHORTCUT Setting the Codec in iMovie
>
> When you export a video to a QuickTime file with iMovie, the standard choices use preset codecs. If you want to select your own codec, use the Expert choice at the bottom of the list, then click the Options button.

Save the video in your project folder; later it will be imported into your Shockwave project and also copied to the Web server.

Streaming Video in Shockwave

Yes, it's possible to use a streaming video source in a Shockwave project. Once the video stream is up and running, you make a **reference movie** for it. This reference movie is like a pointer or alias to the video stream—it's a small file, about 1KB, that contains the information necessary to locate and connect to the stream. By importing this reference movie into your Shockwave project, not only can you see and hear the stream but also your viewers can control and interact with it. You can find more information on streaming video in *The Web Wizard's Guide to Multimedia* and from the online references listed at the end of this chapter.

Preparing 3-D Graphics

Shockwave can use 3-D graphics and allow them to be moved, manipulated, and interacted with in real time. But Director has no capability for creating such elements from scratch. So you must use a 3-D graphics program such as Cinema 4D or Shapeshifter 3D to create the 3-D models. These models, saved in the .w3d format, can then be imported into Director's Cast and from there brought into the Stage and Score and controlled with Lingo scripts. Most 3-D graphics programs, including Maya, 3D Studio Max, Lightwave, Softimage, ShapeShifter 3D, and Cinema 4D, can export their work in the .w3d format.

To see what a 3-D cast member looks like and to understand the 3-D manipulation tools available in Director, download the sample files listed in the Online References section at the end of this chapter, and work with the Director files. Director provides a 3-D shapes window (Figure 3.6) for working with these cast members.

Preparing Shapes

So far in this chapter you have been preparing the media elements outside of the Director–Shockwave development environment. This section and the next briefly describe how to use Director to prepare shapes and vector graphics. These kinds of elements are more easily and efficiently prepared in Director than in other programs.

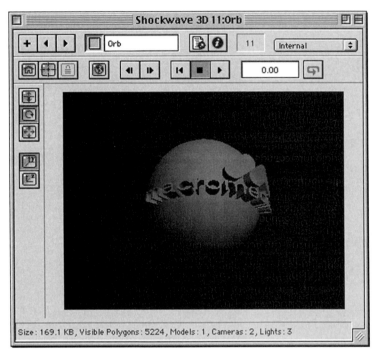

Figure 3.6 Working with 3-D Cast Members

If you plan to use simple, solid shapes in your Shockwave project—rectangles, circles, ovals, squares, and rounded rectangles—create them right in Director; it's a waste of time and data to prepare them in Photoshop and then import them into Director. Director's Tool Palette makes it easy to create such shapes in a way that they take very little space and travel quickly over the Web. Figure 3.7 shows the Tool Palette and the kinds of shapes it can create.

To prepare shapes like these, open Director, then choose Tool Palette from the Window menu. Also make sure the Stage and Cast windows are open. Select a shape tool from the Tool Palette, then click and drag in the Stage to create the shape. You will see the shapes you create show on the Stage and take their places in the Cast window. To make a perfect circle or perfect square, hold down the shift key as you drag the ellipse or rectangle tool.

The color of the shape is set by the color chips in the Tool Palette. The one on top shows the foreground (or fill) color. Set the color *before* drawing the shape. A shape created in Director takes up much less space (less than 300 bytes) than a similar-sized bitmap shape imported from outside (about 5000 bytes). Shape cast members are defined and stored by a small set of numbers that denote the size, shape, and color.

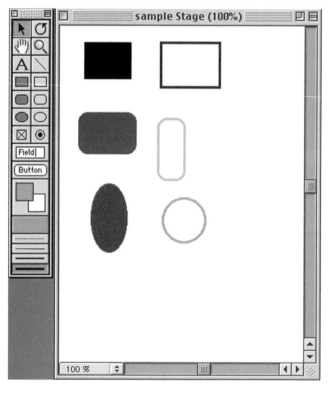

Figure 3.7 Tool Palette and Sample Shapes

Preparing Vector Graphics

A vector graphic shape is even more efficient and can include distortions and gradients, as shown in Figure 3.8. These cast members animate more quickly than bitmaps in Shockwave.

To create a vector shape, open the Vector Shape window from the Window menu. Use the tools on the left to set the color and style of the shape you create. Drag the little square handles to distort the shape. Vector graphics are defined by mathematical formulas that describe the shape, color, and gradient of the cast member.

You can also prepare vector graphics outside Director, with programs such as Macromedia Freehand and Adobe Illustrator, and then import them into your Shockwave project.

You've written the play, set up the stage, hired the actors, and prepared them for the production. Now it's time to get them onto the stage and begin the action. In the next chapter you will learn to put all of these media elements onto the stage.

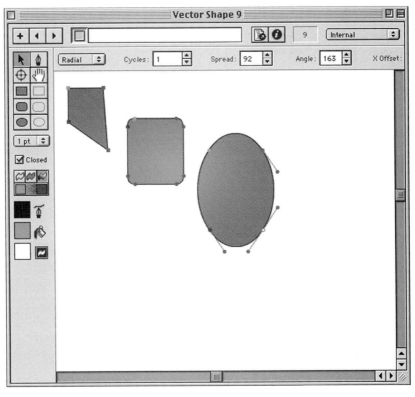

Figure 3.8 Creating Vector Shapes

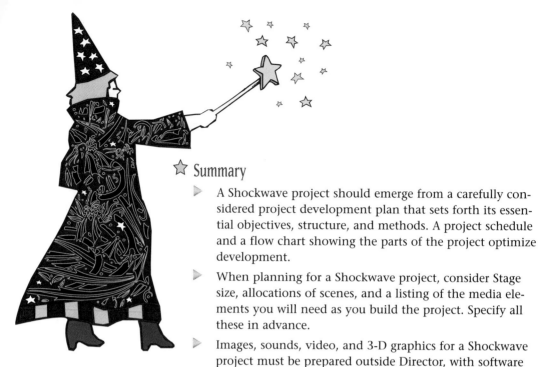

☆ Summary

▷ A Shockwave project should emerge from a carefully considered project development plan that sets forth its essential objectives, structure, and methods. A project schedule and a flow chart showing the parts of the project optimize development.

▷ When planning for a Shockwave project, consider Stage size, allocations of scenes, and a listing of the media elements you will need as you build the project. Specify all these in advance.

▷ Images, sounds, video, and 3-D graphics for a Shockwave project must be prepared outside Director, with software appropriate for each element's type. Each must adhere to certain specifications and must be saved in a format compatible with Director. Shapes and vector graphics can be prepared outside Director or with Director's own shape and vector graphics tools. Text is best prepared in a word-processing program.

☆ Online References

Photoshop information
`http://www.adobe.com/products/photoshop/main.html`

SoundEdit information
`http://macromedia.com/software/sound/`

SoundForge information
`http://www.sonicfoundry.com/products/`
`NewShowProduct.asp?PID=460`

Premiere information
`http://www.adobe.com/products/premiere/main.html`

iMovie information
`http://www.apple.com/imovie/`

Final Cut Pro information
`http://www.apple.com/finalcutpro/`

Streaming video and reference movie instructions
`http://helpqt.apple.com/qtssWebAdminHelpR3/qtssWebAdmin.help/`
`English.lproj/QTSSHelp.htm` (QuickTime Streaming)
`http://www.realnetworks.com/products/servers/plus/index.html`
(RealVideo streaming)

How Shockwave 3D Technology Works
`http://www.howstuffworks.com/shockwave4.htm`

The Basics of Director 3D
`http://www.macromedia.com/support/director/3d_basics.html`

Sources of 3-D sample files
`http://download.macromedia.com/pub/director/3d/3d_for_dir_use`
`rs.sea.hqx` (Macintosh)
`http://download.macromedia.com/pub/director/3d/3d_for_dir_use`
`rs.zip` (Windows)

☆ Review Questions

1. Describe three of the key elements of a development plan for a Shockwave project.

2. List three things that should be considered when setting the Stage size of a Shockwave project.

3. Why are a flow chart and a list of media elements important to a Shockwave project?

4. What roles do markers perform in a Shockwave project?

5. Describe the process of preparing an image file for importing into Director.

6. List the sound file formats that Director can import.

7. Why is the file size of media to be imported into a Shockwave project so important?

8. List four programs that can be used to prepare media files for a Shockwave project, and describe the kinds of media they create.

☆ Hands-On Exercises

1. Write a project development plan for your own Shockwave project. Include all the elements listed in this chapter, except budget and personnel.

2. Draw a flow chart for your Shockwave project, with a rectangle for each scene and lines that show the flow between sections.

3. Open Director, and set the Stage size for your project, taking into consideration the needs of your target audience as described in this chapter.

4. Organize your project into sections, and place a marker in the score for each section. Label the markers as described in this chapter.

5. Prepare two each of the following media types for your project, following the guidelines in this chapter: text, images, sound, video, and shapes. Be sure to use the proper sizes and file formats.

CHAPTER FOUR

Putting the Cast on the Stage

*Life's but a walking shadow, a poor player
that struts and frets his hour upon the stage
and then is heard no more.*

—from *Macbeth*

This chapter places you in the role of a director at the first rehearsal of a play, lining up the actors, arranging the scenery, and putting the players on the stage. You will learn how to import the media elements you have prepared into Director, how to organize and modify them, and how to place them in their proper places on the Stage. As you do this, you will learn to use the Score, the Property Inspector, the Paint window, and other tools provided by the Shockwave development environment. The best way to use this chapter is to build your own Shockwave project as you work through the chapter, importing your own cast members and placing them on the Stage.

◎◎ Chapter Objectives

☆ To learn how to set up the Shockwave development environment for your work

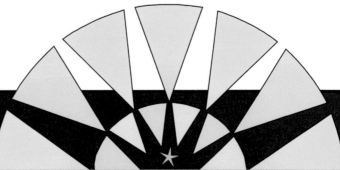

To learn how to import various media elements, how to set and modify the properties of cast members, and how to design the Stage

 To understand the process of placing cast members on the Stage and in the Score

◎◎ Confirming the Setup

Before importing the members of your cast, make sure that the environment is ready for them. In Director, you should have the Stage, Score, and Cast windows open and positioned on your computer's display so you can see all of them.

☆ **TIP**   **Display Size for Director**

The Director environment uses many different windows, which must be used simultaneously in many cases. You need as much space on your computer screen as you can get to fit all these windows. Most Director developers set their display size to its maximum—as many pixels as the system will show. In Windows, choose Display Settings from the Control Panels. On Macintosh, choose the Monitors control panel. Set your display to as many pixels as it will show, and you will find Director easier to use.

Locate all the media elements you have prepared, and place them in a single folder or directory on your hard drive.

Stage Size and Color

You learned about Stage size in Chapter Two; now it's time to confirm that the Stage is set to the correct size for your project. Modify it as necessary by choosing Modify→Movie→Properties from the menu bar. While you are in the Property Inspector for the movie, set the Stage color as well, using the Stage color rectangle next to the paint bucket, as shown in Figure 4.1.

☆ **WARNING**   **Stage Color and Page Color**

If you are going to embed your Shockwave project in a Web page and blend it seamlessly into the background of the page, you want to plan the Stage color carefully. Choose a Stage color that you can duplicate exactly as a Web-page background color using HTML codes. Director's Property Inspector shows the Stage color in hexadecimal notation, which you should make note of and use as the Web-page background color when you embed the Shockwave project. The embedding process is covered in Chapter Eight.

Markers

The Score window for your project should display the markers that set off the scenes, as described in Chapter Two. Make sure the markers are placed where they belong and named properly. You'll use these markers to organize the cast members as you put them on the Stage.

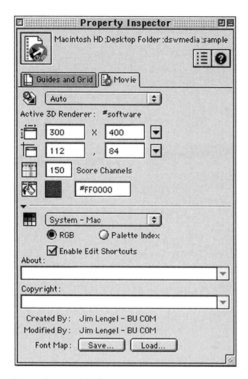

Figure 4.1 Modifying Stage Size and Color

◎◎ Importing the Actors

Now it's time to bring the media elements into the Director programming environment. This is like opening the theater, calling in the actors, and sitting them down backstage. You'll import each element in turn, and as you do they will become cast members for your Shockwave project.

Importing Images, Sound, Video, and 3-D Files

Importing the files you prepared outside Director is easily accomplished, but you must beware the details. Choose File→Import from the menu bar, and look at the Import Files dialog box, shown in Figure 4.2.

Make sure you choose Standard Import from the pop-up menu at the bottom of the Import Files dialog box. This will cause the images and sounds to be brought into the Shockwave file and saved with it onto the Web server. Do not use the Link to External File option—this sets up a pointer to the files, rather than including them in the Shockwave project, and will not produce good results. (Some files, such as digital videos and sounds saved in the `.mov` format, are automatically linked.)

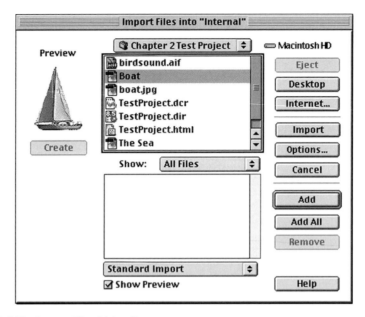

Figure 4.2 The Import Files Dialog Box

☆**TIP**   Can't See the File?

If the file you want to import does not show up in the list in the Import Files dialog box, then the file is not saved in a format Director understands. Go back to the software program in which you prepared the file, follow the directions in Chapter Three, and save the file in the correct format. Table 4.1 shows the formats that Director can import.

Table 4.1 File Formats That Can Be Imported into Director

Type of Media	File Formats	Filename Extensions
Images	JPEG, GIF, PNG, BMP, PICT, TIFF, Photoshop	`.jpg, .gif, .png, .bmp, .pct, .tif, .psd`
Sound	AIFF, Waveform, MP3, Shockwave Audio, Sun Audio, QuickTime, IMA compression	`.aif, .wav, .mp3, .swa, .au, .mov`
Video	QuickTime, AVI	`.mov, .avi`
Animation	Animated GIFs, Flash movies	`.gif, .swf`

When the file is imported, Director will place it automatically into the Cast window, in the next available place. To import into a particular place in the Cast window, select a blank spot, then choose File→Import from the menu bar. In the cast window you will see a thumbnail of the item you imported, unless it's a sound, which has no thumbnail. You'll also see a little icon in the corner of the thumbnail that shows what kind of cast member it is. Table 4.2 shows these icons and the cast member types they represent.

Table 4.2 Cast Member Types and Their Icons

Type	Icon
Bitmap image	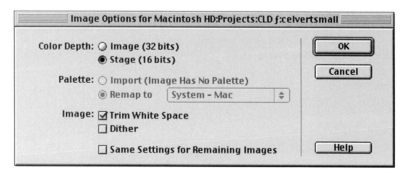
3-D object	
Vector graphic	
Shape	
Sound	
Video	
Flash	
Text	
Field text	

Color Depth

When importing bitmap images, Director may ask you about how much of the image's color information you want to import. The more information you import, the more accurate the color, and the more data in the file. More data translates to more download time over the Web. When given a choice, choose 16-bit color depth, as shown in Figure 4.3—this seems to be the best compromise of quality and file size.

Figure 4.3 Setting Color Depth Before Importing an Image

As you import a series of files into your project, you should save your work every few minutes.

Modifying Images in the Paint Window

Director provides tools for modifying bitmap images you have imported. It's a good idea to inspect each of your images in the Paint window, to make sure they appear as desired. Double-click a bitmap image in the Cast window to see it open in the Paint window. Here you can use the paint tools and modifiers to touch up and alter the image as necessary. Figure 4.4 shows the Paint window and its tools in Director.

Figure 4.4 The Paint Window

You can also use the Paint window to create Shockwave cast members from scratch, using the drawing tools in the palette. These tools are similar to but not exactly the same as the tools in Photoshop. The tools shown on the left side in Figure 4.4 are used as described below.

☆ *Lasso*: Selects portions of the image. Select the lasso, then click and drag to outline your selection. Items selected with the lasso cannot be flipped or distorted.

☆ *Marquee tool*: Selects rectangular portions of the image. Select the marquee, then click and drag across the image to create a rectangular selection. Items selected with the marquee tool can be flipped and distorted with the tools at the top of the Paint window.

☆ *Registration point*: Sets the registration point of the cast member. This is important for animation, as you will learn in Chapter Five.

☆ *Eraser*: Replaces the pixels it drags over with pixels of the background color.

☆ *Hand*: Moves the image within the Paint window. Select the hand, then click and drag on the image to move it.

☆ *Magnifying glass*: Zooms the image view in and out. Select the glass, then click the image to enlarge it. Hold the shift key as you click to zoom out.

☆ *Eyedropper*: Picks up a color from the image. Select the eyedropper, click a spot on the image, and watch its color appear in the foreground color chip.

☆ *Paint bucket*: Fills color in an area of the image. Select the paint bucket, choose a color with the foreground color chip, then click a spot in the image and watch it fill up with the color you chose.

☆ *Text tool*: Paints text on the screen. Select the text tool, click in the Paint window, and type. Double-click on the text tool icon to change the font, size, and style of the text.

☆ *Pencil*: Draws freehand lines one pixel wide. Select the pencil, then click and drag on the image to draw a line. Hold down the shift key as you draw to make straight lines.

☆ *Airbrush*: Spatters paint on the screen. Select the airbrush, then click and drag in the image to make a splash of color. Double-click the airbrush icon to adjust the nature of the splash.

☆ *Paintbrush*: Paints on the screen. Select the paintbrush, then click and drag in the image to make a stroke of color. Double-click the paintbrush icon to adjust the nature of the stroke.

☆ *Arc tool*: Paints arcs on the screen. Select the arc tool, then click and drag in the window to make an arc.

☆ *Line tool*: Creates straight lines. The width of the line is set by the line width buttons described below. Hold down the shift key as you draw to create exact horizontal, vertical, or 45° lines.

☆ *Shape tools*: Create shapes in the Paint window. The three tools on the left create filled shapes, while the three on the right create outlines. Use these tools to create rectangles, ellipses, and many-sided irregular polygons. Holding down the shift key as you use these tools creates perfect squares and circles.

☆ *Gradient colors tool*: Creates an object whose color blends from one to the other. Use this in conjunction with the ink pop-up menu described below.

☆ *Foreground and background color chips*: Set the foreground and background colors. The foreground color is what the paintbrush, pencil, airbrush, and shape tools use. The background color is what appears behind text that you paint on the screen. Click and hold or right-click these chips to change the color.

☆ *Pattern rectangle*: Paints and draws in a pattern or texture, rather than in a solid color. This applies to all painting tools. Click and hold or right-click the pattern rectangle to change the pattern.

☆ *Line width buttons*: Set the width of the line created by the line, arc, and shape tools. Double-click the last button to set larger widths.

☆ *Color depth button*: Sets the color depth. Double-click this button to change the color depth and size of a cast member.

Those are the basic image selection and creation tools. Across the top of the Paint window appear the image modification tools. To use these tools, select all or a part of the image with the marquee tool, then click on one of the modification tools.

☆ *Flip horizontal tool*: Flips the selected part of the image from left to right.

☆ *Flip vertical tool*: Flips the selected part of the image from top to bottom.

☆ *Rotate left tool*: Rotates the selected part of the image 90° counterclockwise.

☆ *Rotate right tool*: Rotates the selected part of the image 90° clockwise.

☆ *Free rotate tool*: Puts handles on the selection, which you can grab with the mouse and move to rotate it.

☆ *Skew tool*: Puts handles on the selection, which you can grab with the mouse and drag to distort it in a parallelogram.

☆ *Warp tool*: Puts handles on the selection, which you can grab with the mouse and drag to distort it by stretching it from each corner.

☆ *Perspective tool*: Puts handles on the selection, which you can grab with the mouse and drag to distort it so it can be seen in perspective.

The Paint window can help you modify existing cast members and create new ones. It also comes in handy when creating simple animations, as you will see in the next chapter.

☆ SHORTCUT **Removing Cast Members**

Unused cast members take up space in your Shockwave project, so it's best to remove them. Simply select the unwanted member in the Cast window and press the delete key (or choose Clear from the Edit menu.)

Importing and Creating Text

There are three ways you can create text in a Shockwave project.

1. *Bitmapped text*. You create bitmapped text (also called painted text) in Photoshop or in Director's Paint window. Bitmapped text works well for big

titles or stylized text. It is really an image, a picture of the words. Once created, it cannot be edited from the keyboard. Use bitmapped text when you want it to act like a graphic.

2. *Rich text.* This is the best way to present static text on the screen for the user to read. But it is not interactive; the user cannot edit it, and you cannot manipulate this text with Lingo. You can edit rich text while you are building your Director project, but once you have made your project into a Shockwave (`.dcr`) file, the text is frozen into place and cannot be changed. With rich text, you need not worry about whether or not the user's computer contains the font you chose. The font is "burned in" when you create the Shockwave file.

3. *Field text.* Use field text for interactive text that you want the user to manipulate or that you want to search, change with Lingo scripts, or develop hypertext with. You can edit field text anywhere and at all times. But be careful: use only system fonts (such as Arial, Helvetica, Courier, Times, Symbol) in field text because these are the only fonts that you know every user will have and the only ones that will translate properly to Windows as well as Macintosh.

As mentioned above, you create bitmapped text in Photoshop or with the text tool in Director's Paint window, a fairly straightforward process. To learn how to create rich text and field text, read on.

Creating Rich Text

Text created in a word processor and saved in Rich Text Format (`.rtf`) can be imported into Director in the normal way. It will appear as a text cast member with its formatting intact. You can also create rich text from scratch in Director, using the Text window (Figure 4.5). Select an unused thumbnail in the Cast window, open the Text window, and begin typing.

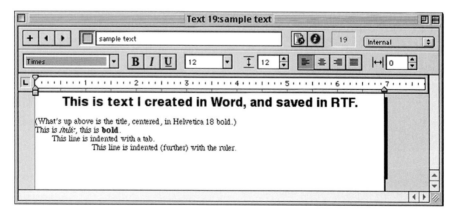

Figure 4.5 The Text Window

Director's Text window works like a word processor. You can type in it; you can select a word, line, or paragraph and change its font, size, or style; you can adjust the line spacing, kerning, and alignment; and you can set the color of the text and the background. Use the ruler at the top to format the margins and indents. The tools and the ways to use them are similar to the same tools in Microsoft Word.

But as you work with your words and paragraphs, keep in mind that text in Shockwave is not the same as text on paper. Avoid long text passages in your Shockwave project. Keep the text cast members short and punchy. People find it difficult to read long columns of text on a computer screen. Keep the line width conducive to good reading: no more than 10 words on a line, adequate line spacing, simple fonts, and a size large enough to see (12 or 14 points in most cases.) People read black text on a plain white background best, so avoid other combinations.

☆**TIP   Text Inspector**

To quickly see and adjust the nature of a text cast member, select it, then choose Window→Inspectors→Text Inspector from the menu bar.

Text from the Text window will be anti-aliased when it appears on the Stage, so the user will not see the jagged edges of the pixels. But this anti-aliasing doesn't work well with text smaller than 12 points, so avoid smaller sizes. To set the color of the text and its background, select the text, and then use the foreground and background color chips in the Tool Palette to change the colors.

Text that you create in the Text window is static text—users can read it in your Shockwave project but cannot interact with it. They can't click on a word to obtain something new or enter their own responses. To create text users can interact with, use the Field window.

Creating Field Text

Field text is interactive text. Open the Field window, and type or paste your text into it. You can use the tools in the Field window to edit and format the text, and you can use the Tool Palette to change the color of the text and its background. A sample of field text is shown in Figure 4.6.

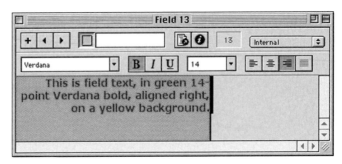

Figure 4.6 Creating Field Text

In Chapters Six and Seven you will learn how to script field text sprites to create interactivity and to input text from the user's keyboard.

Creating 3-D Text

It's easy to create 3-D text for your Shockwave project that can be scripted to animate in space for special effects. Don't use 3-D text for content that you want your viewers to read; use it instead for graphic titles and logos.

To create 3-D text, follow these instructions.

1. Open the Text window, and enter your text. 3-D text works best in large, bold, plain font styles, as shown in Figure 4.7. Format your text as necessary.

2. Open the Property Inspector for this new text cast member by clicking the little blue *i* button at the top of the Text window.

3. Set the display to 3-D mode by using the pop-up menu in the Property Inspector.

4. Open the Shockwave 3-D window from the Window menu.

5. Use the 3-D window tools to modify the 3-D text.

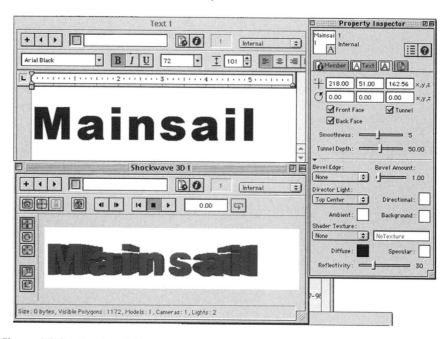

Figure 4.7 Creating 3-D Text

Importing Animations

Although Director's animation tools are first rate, making it easy to create your own animations, Director can also import Flash and GIF animations. Flash animations must be in the `.swf` format, GIFs in the `.gif` format. When imported, they appear in the Cast window with their own icons. When dragged to the Stage they animate in place.

Naming the Cast Members

You have now imported your collection of cast members into Director, and they appear in the Cast window. Like the actors in a drama, these cast members will be easier to identify and work with if you know their names. Assign each of your cast members a unique name. You will use these names later in Lingo scripts, so keep the names short—if possible, a single word. In Figure 4.8, the developer has named the first two cast members and is in the process of naming the third.

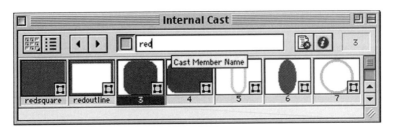

Figure 4.8 Assigning Names to Cast Members

The easiest way to name cast members is to select each cast member in turn in the Cast window and enter the name in the box at the top of the window. Make absolutely certain that no two cast members end up with the same name. To ensure that your names are unique, choose Edit→Find→Cast Member from the menu bar, and then list by name. This will enable you to spot any duplicates.

Setting the Properties of the Cast Members

You can set the manner in which certain cast members appear on the Stage by using the Property Inspector. This is like putting makeup on the actors before they go onstage. Different types of cast members can take different kinds of properties, as shown in Table 4.3.

Designing the Stage

Director gives you ultimate flexibility in how you design the computer's screen. You can put almost anything anywhere you want on the Stage. Here are a few tips that will keep your work elegant and parsimonious.

☆ *Use a plain background.* A solid color background chosen from the Modify→Movie→Properties menu will perform faster than a fancy bitmap file background imported into the Cast window.

☆ *Be consistent.* Design elements that occur over several screens, such as navigation buttons and titles, should appear in the same places. Use similar colors throughout the program.

☆ *Keep it simple.* Avoid visual doodads and gewgaws. Avoid using many different textures and shapes on the same screen. If a visual element is not necessary to the program's function, remove it.

Make navigation obvious. Don't keep the user guessing about how to get around in the program. Keep navigation tools at the same place on every screen.

Table 4.3 Cast Members and Their Properties

Type of Cast Member	Properties You Can Set
Bitmap (paint)	The color palette and whether or not the cast member will highlight when clicked by the user
Field text	The kind of field (adjustable, scrolling, or fixed); whether or not the user can edit it (if used for text entry); and the nature of the field's border, shadows, and margins (using the pop-up menus at the bottom of the Property Inspector)
Text	The framing of the text, the display mode, and the anti-aliasing and kerning of the text (using the pop-up menus)
Vector graphic	The colors, the width of the stroke, and the sizing of the graphic
Shape	The type of shape and whether or not it's filled (using the Property Inspector)
3-D object	The axis position, light, and texture (using the Property Inspector)
Video	The nature of the playback and whether or not to show the controller
Sound	Whether the sound should play once or loop (using the Property Inspector)

◎◎ Placing the Cast on the Stage

The stage is set, and the actors are in the wings awaiting the first rehearsal. Your first task is to block out where the various cast members will appear in one of your scenes. Pick a scene, place the playhead right on the marker, and put the cast members on the Stage. You'll put your background cast members on the Stage first, then move up to the foreground items.

You can get a cast member from the Cast window to the Stage by using either of the following methods.

☆ Drag the cast member directly from the Cast window to its place on the Stage. Notice that it shows up also in the next available channel in the Score.

Drag the cast member from the Cast window into the Score window, and place it into the desired frame and channel. Notice that it shows up in the center of the Stage (except for sound cast members, which have no manifestation on the Stage).

Once the cast member is on the Stage, you can move it around and resize it so it looks the way you want. But avoid resizing large images—if Shockwave has to shrink or stretch an image while running, especially a large image, Shockwave will slow down. Also, remember that when you move a cast member on the Stage, its location is changed *only in that frame*. If you want to move a cast member that stays on the Stage for several frames, you need to select all those frames in the Score before moving the cast member.

★ **WARNING** **Resizing Sprites**

Be careful when resizing bitmap and video sprites on the Stage. These types of sprites perform more predictably and quickly in their original sizes. If you find a sprite too large, resize it in its original form in the Paint window or in the program with which you created it.

Using Sprite Channels in Director's Score Window

When a cast member is on the Stage and in a channel in the Score, it is called a *sprite*. So the cast member in channel 5 is called sprite 5. Sprites in channels with low numbers appear behind sprites with high numbers. You can have many sprites on the Stage at any one time, but the more sprites you have there at once, the slower the program will run.

The cast members that appear at the back of the Stage—backgrounds and scenery—should be dragged in first and set into the low-numbered sprite channels. But leave sprite channel 1 empty for now—you may need this later to slip in a sprite that appears behind everything.

When you drag the cast member into the Stage or the Score, it puts itself into several frames, across the entire scene from marker to marker, as shown in Figure 4.9.

Notice in Figure 4.9 that the boat is selected on the Stage. Its representation in the Score is also selected. The boat on the Stage is called sprite 3 because it is in sprite channel 3, in front of the sea but behind the bird. If you were to move the boat from sprite channel 3 to sprite channel 1, it would disappear—it would be behind the sea (sprite 2), which is larger and covers it up.

★ **WARNING** **Default Sprite Length**

If no markers are defined in the Score, Director will put the sprite across 28 frames in the Score. That's the default duration. If a marker is present, the sprite will be stretched to the frame just before the next marker. You can set the default duration by choosing File→Preferences→Sprite from the menu bar.

At this point in the process, you are building the static prototype of a chunk of your Shockwave project—all the pieces are there, but they don't do anything yet.

In Chapter Five you'll make these sprites move, and in Chapter Six you'll make them interact.

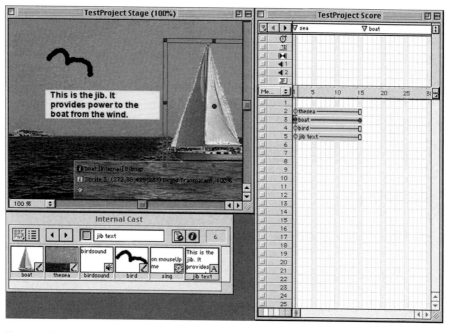

Figure 4.9 Sprites in the Score and on the Stage

⭐ **SHORTCUT Cast Member Number versus Sprite Number**

Notice that the boat in Figure 4.9 is cast member 1, but on the Stage it is sprite 3. This is an important distinction. Note also that the boat, when selected on the Stage, shows you its information right under it: cast member name, sprite number, location, and ink. If you don't see this information for a selected sprite on your Stage, choose View→Sprite Overlay from the menu bar.

Aligning Sprites

You may wish your sprites to appear in an exact position on the Stage or to appear in line with other sprites. Director provides two tools to help with this: a grid and an alignment tool. The grid blocks out the entire Stage in a regular pattern of rectangles, into which you place your sprites, while the alignment tool lines up sprites that are already on the Stage.

The Grid

To see the grid, choose View→Guides and Grid→Show Grid from the menu bar. You will see a grid placed over the Stage. The user will not see this grid; it's just for you. It performs a function similar to the bits of fluorescent tape attached to the stage that actors use to line themselves up during various scenes of a play. The default grid is 64 pixels square; you can adjust this under View→Guides and Grid→Settings.

The grid serves as a place to line up your sprites. It's especially useful in guaranteeing that a sprite will appear in the exact same spot in all scenes. If you like, you can choose View→Guides and Grid→Snap to Grid, which will cause sprites placed near a gridline to snap automatically to the grid.

The Align Tool

Use the align tool to line up a series of sprites with each other or relative to the Stage. First select the sprites you want to align. Then choose Modify→Align from the menu bar. You will see an alignment palette with two pop-up menus, one for horizontal alignment, the other for vertical, as illustrated in Figure 4.10. Choose the kind of alignment you want, and then click the Align button at the bottom of the palette. You will see the selected sprites line up with each other.

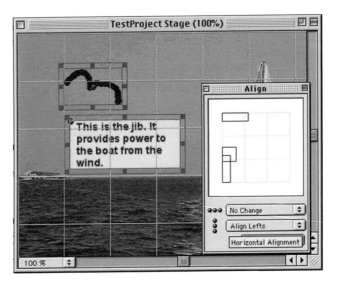

Figure 4.10 Aligning Sprites

Resizing Sprites

Once you have placed a cast member on the Stage, you can resize the sprite by selecting it and then dragging the handles on its corners. If you hold down the shift key as you drag, the sprite will resize proportionally. Resizing a sprite does not affect the size of the cast member—if you were to drag the boat from the Cast window into the Stage in another scene, it would appear in its original size.

Resizing bitmap, vector, and shape members works as expected and can be accomplished without penalty. But avoid resizing video cast members—the playback performance will suffer if the video is displayed at anything other than its original size. When you resize a text or field cast member, the box will change shape, but the text itself will not get any smaller or larger; it will just move around in the box. If you want to resize the text itself (and thus the overall size of the text sprite), select it, open the Text or Field window, and change the size of the text there.

Looking Ahead

Your cast is on the Stage, in their places from back to front, top to bottom, and side to side. You've created only one scene so far; you can build the others the same way. It's best to build just two or three scenes now, then make them move and interact. Once you've mastered motion and action for these first prototype scenes, you'll find it easy to build the rest of the scenes later. So take five, and be ready to animate these sprites in the next chapter.

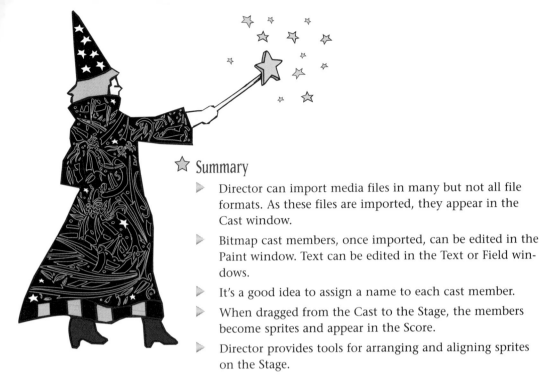

☆ Summary

▷ Director can import media files in many but not all file formats. As these files are imported, they appear in the Cast window.

▷ Bitmap cast members, once imported, can be edited in the Paint window. Text can be edited in the Text or Field windows.

▷ It's a good idea to assign a name to each cast member.

▷ When dragged from the Cast to the Stage, the members become sprites and appear in the Score.

▷ Director provides tools for arranging and aligning sprites on the Stage.

☆ Online References

Director Basics tutorial
`http://www.macromedia.com/software/director/productinfo/tutorials/gettingstarted/`

Guidance for implementing a multimedia project
`http://macromedia.com/support/director/how/expert/manage/managemm03.html#0008`

Information on importing vector and EPS files into Director
`http://www.macromedia.com/support/director/ts/documents/vector_import.htm`

Media types that Director can import
`http://www.macromedia.com/support/director/ts/documents/media_files.htm`

☆ Review Questions

1. Describe the process of importing a media element into Director.

2. List at least six types of files that Director can import.

3. Describe the capabilities of the Paint window in Director.

4. Explain the three types of text that Director can handle and when each would be used.

5. What should be considered when designing the Stage for a Shockwave project?

6. Explain the difference between cast member numbers and sprite channel numbers.

7. Describe the process of putting a cast member onto the Stage.

8. How do you align and resize sprites?

☆ Hands-On Exercises

1. Create the following media elements from scratch in Director:
   ★ A bitmap image in the Paint window
   ★ A shape image with the Tool Palette
   ★ A paragraph of rich text
   ★ A paragraph of field text
   ★ A word in 3-D text

2. Name each of the cast members in your project.

3. Use the Property Inspector to modify at least five of your cast members.

4. For two new scenes of your project, put the cast members onto the Stage as described in this chapter. Ensure that they appear in the appropriate sprite channels. Include as many different kinds of cast members as possible.

5. Use the grid or the alignment tool to align some of your sprites. Also, resize at least two sprites.

CHAPTER FIVE

Making Things Move

Doubt that the sun doth move,
doubt truth to be a liar,
but never doubt I love.

—from *Hamlet*

Movement is a key aspect of many Shockwave projects. This chapter teaches you how to create animation for your Web site, from a ball that rolls across the Stage to titles that zoom in to an actor who moves his lips as he speaks. You can include many different types of animation in your Shockwave project. And since the roots of Director are in animation, you will find that the tools and techniques for making things move are unsurpassed. Begin this chapter by thinking about where animation can enhance your own Shockwave project, and then build several different kinds of animation into your project as you work through the chapter.

Chapter Objectives

⭐ To explore the different types of animation you can include in a Shockwave project

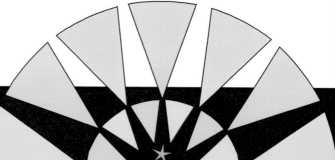

☆ To understand basic animation concepts

☆ To learn how to create a simple path animation

☆ To learn how to create a simple parts-in-place animation

☆ To learn how to create and animate a film loop

☆ To learn how to set up animation that users can initiate

☆ To learn how to create animation from Director's built-in behaviors

☆ To discover hints and tips for creating animation

☆ To learn how to create rollover, mouseDown, and moveable sprite animations through scripting

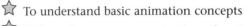 Types of Animation

Anything that moves on the screen can be considered an animation. And since objects can move in many different ways, and for different purposes, the concept of animation is key to making the most of Shockwave. You may not need all of these different types of animation in your own project; nonetheless, you should understand and build each type as part of your Shockwave education. The first part of this chapter describes the different types of animation you can create in Shockwave; subsequent sections take you through the process of building each kind.

Path Animation

In this type of animation, an object appears to move across the screen, along a path set for it by the developer. It might be a plane flying across the sky, a word flying in from the top to form a title, or a ball bouncing along the bottom of the window. Though the illustrations on the pages of this book cannot move, you can see in Figure 5.1 what a simple path animation looks like.

Figure 5.1 Simple Path Animation

Figure 5.1 shows three frames of a 20-frame animation, including the first and last frames and one from the middle. In the first frame, the boat appears at the right; the boat then moves across to the left over 20 frames of the Score. The boat is following a path defined for it by the developer. Each time this animation plays, the boat follows exactly the same path.

Any sprite can be animated: a bitmap such as the boat, words in text, shapes, vector graphics, even video cast members and entire paragraphs of text. The path can be straight, curved, or full of circular loops and bounces. This chapter shows you how to create simple path animations.

Parts-in-Place Animation

In this type of animation, the object itself stays still, but parts of it appear to be in motion. The bird flaps its wings. The cartoon character moves his lips as he talks. The wheels on the tractor rotate in place. Certain key parts of the object move, but the object itself stays in the same place. Figure 5.2 shows a simple parts-in-place animation.

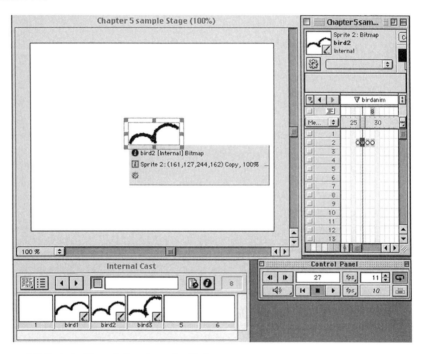

Figure 5.2 Parts-in-Place Animation of a Bird

As you can see from Figure 5.2, this animation is made up of three different cast members: bird1, bird2, and bird3. When displayed in rapid succession over and over, it looks as if the bird is flapping its wings. You could use the same technique to create three different mouths for the talker (one with lips tightly closed, a second partly open, and a third fully open) or three wheels for the tractor (each at a different angle of rotation). Parts-in-place animation can move the hands of a clock, the flames of a candle, the wink of an eye, or the swing of a bell. You'll learn how to add parts-in-place animation to your Shockwave project in this chapter.

Animation Synchronized with Sound

When an animation is synchronized with its sound, the effect can be profound and highly effective. Listen to the tolling of the bell as you watch it swing through its arc. Hear the man speak as his lips move. Although the sound is developed separately and is not part of the animated object itself, this chapter shows you how to set up this synchronization in the Score.

Film Loop Animation

Imagine the bird, with wings flapping in place, also moving across the screen. Imagine the ball rotating as it bounces along the bottom. This combination of parts-in-place and path animation is easy to include in your Shockwave project and easy to develop. You can combine a series of frames from a parts-in-place animation into a single cast member called a **film loop**. This film loop animates wherever you place it on the Stage, and you can move it in a path animation like any other sprite. The result is a complex animation that you will learn how to create later in this chapter.

Lingo-Scripted Animation

The animations described so far are all controlled by the Score—the action takes place frame-by-frame, the object changing its location as the movie plays over time. Objects can also be moved by Lingo scripts that put the object in a different location on the Stage. Often embedded in loops that move the object just a few pixels at each iteration, Lingo-scripted animations can create interactive animations that flow from user activity or relationships to other objects on the Stage. Lingo scripts are also used to create objects that move randomly, in unpredictable ways that mimic natural behavior, as a honeybee hovering around a blossom.

Since creating this kind of animation relies on complex scripting, we will include it in Chapter Seven, after you've learned how to write Lingo scripts.

Size and Rotation

Picture the title of your Shockwave project appearing first as a barely perceptible dot in the center of the screen and growing slowly to become readable, then growing further to fill the screen. This is often called **zooming text**, but in reality it is another form of simple animation. The title is actually a single sprite that at the beginning of the sequence appears at a very small size, growing gradually larger until at the end it appears full-size. You can also use this technique of changing the size of a sprite over time (in the opposite direction) to make the bird appear to fly off into the distance. This gradual change in size over time is easy to create in Director.

A similar technique creates changes in a sprite's rotation over time. You might use this for a rolling ball, a spinning wheel, or a cartoon man doing cartwheels. The rotation of a sprite is a property you can easily modify (and thus animate) in the Score or with Lingo scripts. You will learn how to create these kinds of animations later in this chapter.

Built-in Behaviors

Director provides built-in, prewritten scripts that can help you create certain kinds of animation, such as random movement around the Stage, "wafting" up from the bottom to the top of the Stage, or rotating in place in a regular manner. You'll learn how to use these behaviors also.

Other Types of Animation

Introduced in this chapter are three additional forms of animation based on user interaction: rollover actions, mousedown actions, and moveable sprites. A **rollover animation** occurs when the user passes the pointer over an object and observes a change in the object he or she rolled over. If the user sees a change in the object when pressing the mouse down on it, this is called a **mouseDown animation**. If the user can click and drag an object around the screen, it is called a **moveable sprite**.

☆**TIP**   **Flash Animation**

Macromedia Flash is a great program for creating animations. *The Web Wizard's Guide to Flash* can teach you how to do this. You can import Flash animations into Director and incorporate them into your Shockwave projects. Simply create the animation with Flash, save it in the `.swf` file format, and then import this file into Director. The Flash animation appears as a cast member, one that will animate when it appears on the Stage.

◎◎ Animation Concepts

Location and Time

The two key concepts in animation are *location* and *time*. An object that changes its location over time is animated. In Shockwave, a sprite's location is determined by its horizontal and vertical coordinates on the Stage. Time is determined, in most cases, by the progress from frame to frame through the Score. The farther a sprite moves in each unit of time, the faster it animates.

Most Shockwave projects run at 30 frames per second. That is the default speed in Director, and unless you change it your movie will proceed through each frame in a 30th of a second. So if you want a sprite to move across the Stage in about 2 seconds (a medium-fast animation), and if the Stage is 420 pixels wide, then the sprite needs to move about 200 pixels per second. If the movie is running at 30 frames per second, then the sprite must move about 7 pixels in each frame (7 pixels per frame × 30 frames per second × 2 seconds = 420 pixels, the width of the Stage). Figure 5.3 shows how this animation would look in the Score and on the Stage.

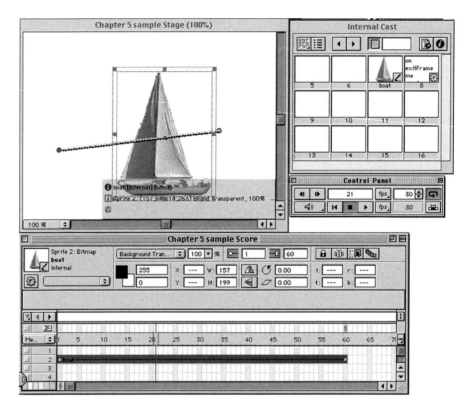

Figure 5.3 Animation Over Time and Location

To make the sprite move faster, reduce the number of frames in the animation while moving it the same total distance across the screen, thus increasing the movement in each frame. In Figure 5.3, the yellow dots on the path would become further apart. The opposite would be true for a slower animation, requiring more frames to move the same total distance.

Tweening

A third key concept in animation is *tweening*. This comes from the word *between*. In Figure 5.3, the boat appears near the right of the screen in frame 10, 257 pixels across the screen. The boat appears in the center of the screen in frame 30, 117 pixels across the screen, so it moved a total distance of 140 pixels over the intervening frames. Since there are 20 frames between frame 10 and frame 30, the boat must move about 7 pixels in each frame. This dividing up of the total movement through the intervening frames is called tweening. In most cases, Director can create the *tweens*—the individual frame locations—automatically if you set the first and last frames of the animation.

Tweening works not only with location but also with brightness, rotation, and size—for instance, as the movie proceeds from frame to frame, the size of the sprite can change gradually from 32 pixels square to 200 pixels square, or the brightness of the sprite (called the *blend* in Director) can change over time from invisible to fully present.

Fixed versus Random Animation

A path animation is fixed—every time the animation occurs, it follows the same path and appears identical to the viewer. Another type of animation is possible in Shockwave, in which the sprite moves at random around or across the screen, following a different path each time the animation occurs. This kind of animation is created with a Lingo script that resets the location of the sprite to a random horizontal and vertical coordinate in each frame. You will learn how to create random scripted animations in Chapter Seven.

◎◎ Creating Path Animation

In this section, you will learn to animate a sprite across the Stage, to adjust its path, to synchronize it with sound, and to change its size and rotate it.

Animating a Single Sprite Along a Path

The simplest animation consists of a single sprite moving across the Stage. Follow the steps below to create such an animation.

1. Determine the number of frames you need for your animation. For a simple sprite to move across the Stage, you might need 60 frames. The sprite in Figure 5.3, for instance, covers 60 frames. The larger the number of frames, the smoother the movement will appear. So if you want a basketball to drop from the top to the bottom of the Stage, a distance of 480 pixels, you should allow at least 48 frames for this to happen. That's about ten pixels per frame, enough to fool the eye into perceiving continuous motion.

2. Use the Paint window to create a simple sprite. Keep it small and simple for now. It will appear in the Cast window.

3. Drag the cast member to the Stage, and place it on one side or the other, where you want the animation to begin. In the Score, drag out the sprite to cover about 30 frames or the number you have planned for this animation.

4. To define the path on the Stage, position the cursor over the registration point of the sprite. This point is marked with a green dot. The cursor will turn white to indicate you're on the center. Click and drag the sprite across the Stage. A line will form, showing the path of animation.

5. Test your animation by using the Control Panel to rewind to the beginning and then to play your animation. You should see the sprite move. The yellow line is the path of the animation, and each dot on the yellow line indicates one frame. Move the playhead through the Score, and you will see each dot become selected on the Stage along with its corresponding frame in the Score.

6. To adjust the path of the animation, select a frame of the animation in the Score. Watch its corresponding dot on the path become selected. Now click and drag that selected dot on the Stage to a new location. The path will move along with it. Repeat this process for other frames in the animation, going back and forth between Score and Stage. The modified path might look something like Figure 5.4.

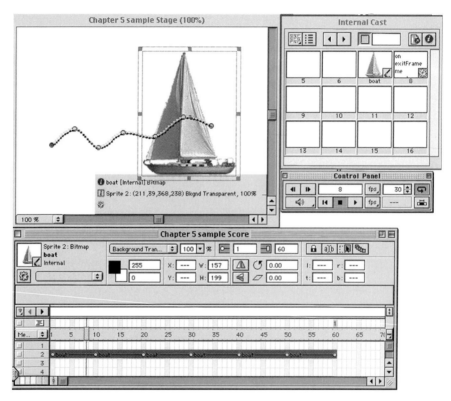

Figure 5.4 Modified Animation Path

Rewind to the beginning of the modified animation and play it. You will notice that if you stretch the path too far, the motion will seem jerky and unnatural. Keep the path smooth and consistent and it will work better.

☆ SHORTCUT **Need More Frames?**

Many animations need more frames than you think to appear smooth and natural. To add more frames to an existing path animation, simply click the last frame of the sprite, and drag it out 15 or 20 frames. Replay the animation to see if it improves.

Real-Time Recording of a Path

You can also create an animation by dragging the sprite around the screen along the desired path and letting Director record the motion. Follow these steps.

1. Place the cast member on the Stage at the location where the animation will begin.

2. Select the sprite on the Stage.

3. Choose Control→Real-Time Recording from the menu bar.

4. Click and drag the sprite along the path you wish it to take.

5. When the path is finished, release the mouse.

6. Play the movie, and see the Sprite move.

7. To see the path you created, select the sprite in the Score.

8. You can modify the path by using the method described in Step 6 above.

Synching the Sound

To create a sound that brings a sense of realism to your animation, create or import a sound that's the same length as or shorter than your animation. The sound will appear in the Cast window. Drag the sound from the Cast window into one of the sound channels in the Score, and stretch it out so that it covers the same frames as the animation, as shown in Figure 5.5.

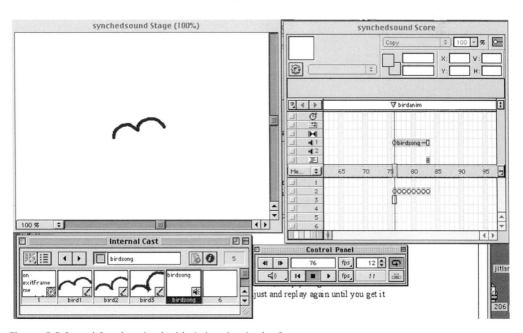

Figure 5.5 Sound Synchronized with Animation in the Score

Rewind to the beginning of the animation and play it. If the sound needs to come a little earlier or later to synchronize exactly with the animation, simply drag the sound in the Score forward or back a few frames, replay, and adjust and replay again until you get it right.

☆TIP   **Multimedia on Your Computer**

To hear the sound you have just synchronized with your animation, you need headphones or speakers for your computer. Turn up the sound volume so that you can hear it. Whenever you use Director on your computer to create Shockwave projects, make sure that the sound is working and that the video display is set to 16-bit color or better.

☆WARNING **Length of Sound**

When you place a sound in one of the sound channels in the Score, make sure you lay the sound out in enough frames to hear it all. A one-second sound clip needs 30 frames to play in its entirety if you're using the default setting of 30 frames per second.

Changing Size and Rotation

When creating the simple path animation, you tweened the location of the sprite across 30 or 40 frames—Director automatically created the progressive locations of the sprites from frame to frame. You can also easily tween the size or rotation of the sprite you have just animated. Here's how.

1. In the Score, click the last frame of the animation you just created.

2. Select the animated sprite.

3. Open the Property Inspector.

4. To rotate this sprite, enter the number of degrees in the rotation field in the Property Inspector (Figure 5.6).

5. To change the size, enter new numbers for the height and width.

This will set the rotation or size of the sprite in the last frame of the animation and tween the frames in between. To see the effect, rewind to the beginning of the animation and play it.

By this same method, you can also change the blend of the sprite over several frames. The blend, which can range from 0 to 100, represents the transparency of the sprite. A sprite with a blend of 0 is invisible; a blend of 50 makes it translucent so that the background shows through; and a blend of 100 is a fully opaque sprite. You can set the blend in the sprite's Property Inspector.

Path animation is the easiest form to create in Director. You just built the animation of a single sprite; by the same method you can animate many sprites simultaneously, each in its own sprite channel, all in the same set of frames, all moving in different directions, along different paths.

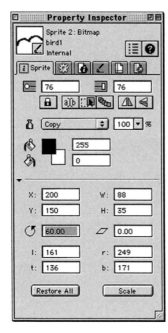

Figure 5.6 Setting the Size and Rotation of a Sprite in the Property Inspector

◎◎ Creating Parts-in-Place Animation

Picture a bird sitting on a branch flapping its wings. The bird itself does not change position; only the wings move. And they don't move far—they simply flap up and down a few pixels at each stroke. You will learn first how to create this parts-in-place animation and then how to combine it with path animation so the bird flies, wings flapping, across the screen.

Setting Up a Parts-in-Place Animation

To create such an animation, you will draw a simple bird, duplicate it, and then modify the duplicate by rotating its wings. Follow these steps.

1. In the Paint window, draw a picture of a bird. A small bird distinct against a plain white background will work best for this exercise, such as the bird shown in Figure 5.7.

2. Use the lasso tool to select the bird. Copy this bird.

3. Click the + button in the Paint window to create a new paint cast member. Into this blank window paste the bird you just copied.

4. Use the rectangular marquee tool to select one of this new bird's wings. (Don't use the lasso tool.)

5. Select the rotation tool in the Paint window just above the picture. See the little squares appear at the corner of the selection rectangle.

6. Drag one of these little squares to rotate the wing. Rotate it about 30 degrees, no more. Click elsewhere in the Paint window to save the rotation.

7. Use the rectangular marquee tool to select the other wing. Rotate this wing about 30 degrees, just as you rotated the first one.

8. You now have two birds in the Cast window, one after the other (Figure 5.8). Use the arrow buttons at the top left of the Paint window to switch back and forth between the two birds. Do the wings seem to flap?

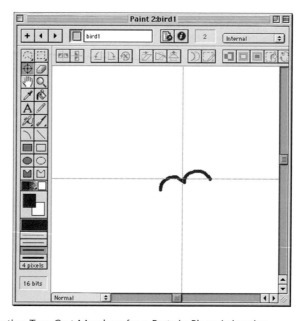

Figure 5.7 Creating Two Cast Members for a Parts-in-Place Animation

These two cast members, when placed into the Score in adjacent frames, one after the other, will create the impression of animation. Here's how to put them on the Stage.

1. Drag the first bird from the Cast window to the Score. Notice that it appears in the center of the Stage.

2. In the Score, set the sprite to occupy two frames by dragging its last frame.

3. Select the next frame in the Score.

4. Drag the second bird from the Cast window to the Score, in the same sprite channel as the first. It will also appear in the center of the Stage.

5. Set the sprite of the second bird to occupy two frames.

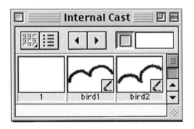

Figure 5.8 Two Cast Members in the Cast Window

6. The two bird sprites in the Score should look like those shown in Figure 5.9.

7. In the Control Panel, set the movie to loop. Rewind and play the frames you just created. You should see the bird flap its wings continuously in the center of the Stage.

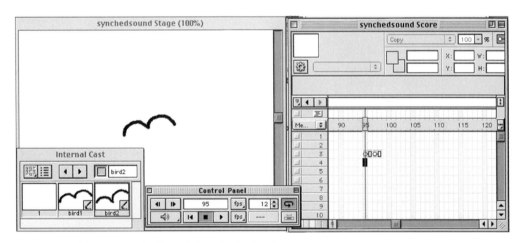

Figure 5.9 Building a Parts-in-Place Animation in the Score

The four frames you created can be copied and pasted to form a longer string of frames to make the animation last exactly as long as you want. Simply select all four frames in the Score, copy them, select the next blank frame, and paste. Do this as many times as necessary. (For example, if your movie is running at the default rate of 30 frames per second, you need to create 60 frames for 2 seconds of flapping bird.)

☆ **SHORTCUT Onion Skinning**

To help you create cast members that are just slightly different from one another, Director includes a feature called **onion skinning**, which allows you to see a translucent representation of the preceding sprites in the Paint window as you are working on the next sprite. To use this feature, open the second cast member in the animation series in the Paint window. Choose View→Onion Skin from the menu bar. Watch the Onion Skin palette open. Click the leftmost button in the palette to turn on onion skinning. You will see a translucent version of the previous sprite in the Paint window.

Creating Parts-in-Place Animation

Setting the Registration Points

Does your bird seem to move up and down or from side to side as it flaps its wings? That's because the registration points of the two bird cast members are not in the same place. Each cast member has a registration point, most often at the center or at the upper-left corner, which is used to indicate the sprite's location on the Stage. Here's how to set the registration point of a paint cast member:

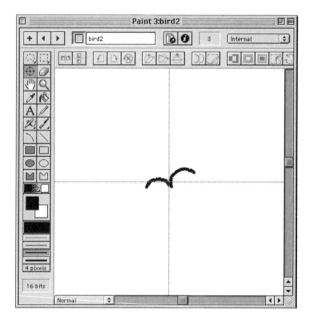

Figure 5.10 Setting the Registration Point of a Cast Member

1. Open your first bird in the Paint window.

2. Select the registration point tool, as shown in Figure 5.10.

3. You will see two lines, one vertical and one horizontal. Their intersection indicates this cast member's registration point.

4. Click the arrow at the upper left of the Paint window to see the second bird. Is its registration point in exactly the same spot on the bird?

5. If not, reset it by clicking the correct spot. (You may find it easier to match the point exactly if you zoom in on the image, by choosing Zoom in from the View menu.)

With the registration points identical, replay the animation. The bird should remain stationary as it flaps its wings.

Modifying the Animation

To move the animated bird to another place on the Stage, first select all its frames in the Score, and then on the Stage drag it to its new location. To slow the rate of flapping, reduce the frame rate of your movie in the Control Panel.

Creating More Complex Animations

A parts-in-place animation like this can be used to animate such things as opening doors, talking mouths, and winking eyes. While the bird in this example uses only two different cast members, a more complex animation might require three or four different images. No matter how complex, the method is the same.

1. Create the cast members, each slightly different from the next.

2. Set the registration points of the cast members.

3. Drag the cast members into the Score in subsequent frames.

4. Test the animation by playing the movie.

Next, you will learn to combine the parts-in-place animation with path animation, to make the bird fly across the screen as its wings flap. You will begin by making the flapping wings animation into a film loop.

◎◎ Creating a Film Loop

Combining Animation Frames into a Film Loop

A film loop is a series of animation frames converted into a single cast member. You can then use this film loop cast member like any other cast member, for example, you can animate it along a path. To learn this process, you will turn the bird you created earlier into a film loop and then animate it along a path. Follow these steps.

1. Drag the first bird from the Cast window into a frame in the Score.

2. Drag the second bird from the Cast window to the next frame in the Score.

3. Set the ink of these sprites to Background Transparent or Matte, as appropriate.

4. Select these two frames in the Score, as shown in Figure 5.11.

5. Choose Film Loop under the Insert menu.

6. Enter a name for the film loop, such as `flying bird`.

You will see a new cast member appear in the Cast window. This is the film loop that contains the flapping wings animation. Double-click the film loop to see it play. At this time, you should also remove the sprites in the Score that you used to create the film loop—they were temporary and are no longer needed. (But don't remove the Cast members from the Cast window.) Next, you will animate this film loop cast member along a path.

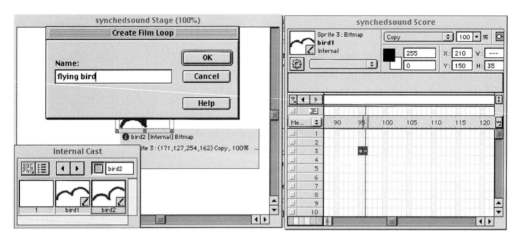

Figure 5.11 Creating a Film Loop

☆**TIP**   **Test Incrementally**

As you make each change, test the movie by choosing Play from the Control menu. By testing the movie incrementally like this, you can fix small problems as they occur. If you wait until later, you'll have a harder time finding where you made an error.

Animating the Film Loop

Following the steps you learned earlier to build a path animation, animate the film loop cast member you just created. Here is a summary of the steps.

1. Drag the film loop cast member to one side of the Stage.

2. In the Score, stretch out the sprite to cover enough frames for a smooth animation, at least 30.

3. Rewind to the first frame of the animation.

4. In the Stage, click the registration point of the sprite and drag it across the Stage.

5. See the yellow line that indicates the path, with a dot for each frame.

6. Play the animation to test it. The bird should appear to fly across the Stage.

7. Modify the path of the animation, as described earlier in this chapter, to make the bird's flight more natural.

The powerful combination of parts-in-place animation, a film loop, and path animation can bring complex movement into your Shockwave project. And you're not restricted to one animation at a time—as the bird flies, the sun can rise, the boat can sail on the sea, and the fish can jump in the waves. Practice your animation skills by creating some animations for your own Shockwave project.

☆**WARNING** **Slow Animations**

Animating small sprites, a few at a time, can be handled by most computers. But to animate large sprites, especially at high color depths, requires significant processing speed and a robust video display system. Some slower computers will not be able to play such an animation at the desired frame rate. The animation will slow down and appear jumpy. If this happens, try animating only a few smaller sprites at a time, with low color depth.

◎◎ Creating User-Initiated Animation

The animations you have created so far are automatic—they occur whenever the movie plays. A more interactive way to use animation is to let the user initiate it. In this example, you will turn the bird animation you just created into one that flies only when the user clicks it.

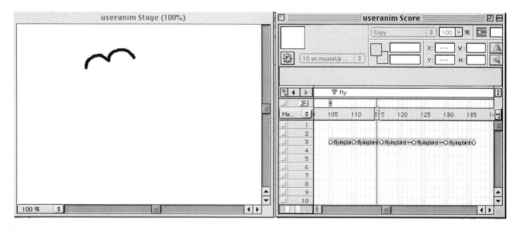

Figure 5.12 Score from a User-Initiated Animation

Your animation in the Score probably looks something like Figure 5.12—but not exactly. In Figure 5.12, you see the addition of user-initiated animation. The animation runs from frame 105 to frame 136. However, notice in this illustration the marker at frame 106 and the script in frame 105. This marker and this script, along with another script that we will attach to the bird, are what enable this user-initiated animation. Here's how it works.

☆ The script in the script channel of frame 105 stops the forward motion of the playhead and keeps it at frame 105. As a result, the bird does not move.

☆ When the user clicks on the bird, a script on the bird sprite sends the playhead to the marker **fly**, and thus through frames 106-136, so that the bird appears to fly.

Follow the steps below to modify your bird animation in the same way.

1. Set up the marker. In the second frame of your animation, create a marker by clicking in the marker area at the top of the Score. Name the marker `fly`.

2. Write the frame script. Double-click the script channel in the first frame of your animation. This will open a script window. Into this window, type the following script.

```
on exitframe
   go to the frame
end
```

This script causes the movie to play this first frame over and over—every time it tries to exit the frame in its inexorable progress to the next frame, it is sent back to the frame it's in—an endless loop.

☆ **TIP   Writing Scripts**

You may notice as you opened these script windows that Director had begun to do your work for you by writing part of the script. This is normal; it is Director's way of anticipating commonly used actions. You need only complete the script as illustrated.

3. Write the sprite script on the bird. Select the bird on the Stage. Choose Modify→Sprite→Script from the menu bar. This will open a Script window. Type this script.

```
on mouseUp
   go to "fly"
end
```

This script sends the playhead to the marker `fly` whenever the user clicks on the bird. (A click actually contains two events: a mouseDown event when the user presses down on the mouse, and a mouseUp event when she or he lets go. Try it—you will feel and hear two clicks.)

4. Test the animation. Place the playhead in the first frame of your animation. Use the Control Panel to play it. (Nothing happens.) Now click the bird and watch it fly once across the screen.

This is but one of the many ways to create a user-initiated animation. Later in this book, as you become more familiar with scripting, you will learn how to create more interactive animations.

◎◎ Using Built-in Animation Behaviors

Path animation and parts-in-place animation are not the only ways to make things move in your Shockwave project. Director provides a library of prescripted animations called **behaviors** that you can invoke without writing your own script from scratch. Here's how to assign one of these animation behaviors to a sprite.

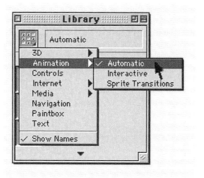

Figure 5.13 Assigning Animation Behavior

1. Use the Paint window to create a new sprite. Place it near the center of the Stage.

2. Find the behavior you want to use. Choose Library from the Window menu. This opens the collection of built-in behaviors. Click the button, then choose Animation→Automatic as shown in Figure 5.13. Now scroll down the list in the Library palette until you find an animation you'd like to try.

3. Assign the animation to the sprite. Drag the icon of the built-in animation to the sprite. Click OK to leave the parameters as they are. This sprite now has a new script. You can see it by selecting the sprite and then choosing Modify→Sprite→Script from the menu bar.

4. Try the animation. Set the movie to play in the Control Panel and watch the sprite move. Assign some other automatic behaviors to see how they work. Try changing some of the parameters to modify the behavior.

As you can see, these are complex scripts for seemingly simple animations. But they work, and you may find these built-in behaviors can help you develop exactly the effect you need for your Shockwave project. But beware—these scripts are very difficult to understand and almost impossible to modify. So use these behaviors with care.

Hints and Tips on Animation

Here are some guidelines for creating good animation:

☆ Large objects do not animate smoothly—there are too many pixels to move at once. Animate small objects for best results.

☆ You can create several simultaneous animations, but not so many that you slow down the movie.

☆ You can animate text as well as graphic objects on the screen.

☆ Placing an appropriate sound effect into a sound channel, across the same frames as your animation, adds realism.

☆ Don't animate things, especially text, unless there is a reason for it.

☆ Use plenty of frames for your animation. Try to keep frame-to-frame movement under 10 pixels.

☆ Real-world animators spend hours creating lifelike animation with Director. Do not expect to duplicate their craft in one lesson.

◎◎ Creating Scripted Animation

With scripts, you can create other forms of animation in your Shockwave project. You can make a sprite change form when the pointer rolls over it. You can make it change again when the user clicks it. These kinds of small animations make your project seem more responsive to the user. You can also create sprites that the user can move with the mouse. These require a bit of scripting, but as you've seen, simple scripting is easy to accomplish. Follow the instructions below to build each of these animations.

Creating Rollover Animation

In this example you'll create a red button that turns blue when the mouse rolls over it. Follow these steps.

1. Use the Paint window or the shape tools to create a round red cast member, such as the one shown in Figure 5.14. This will be cast member 1 in the Cast window.

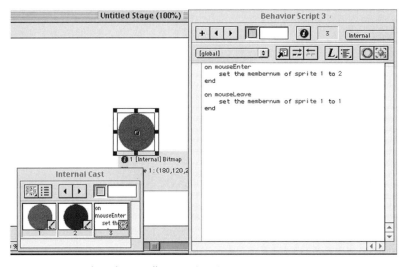

Figure 5.14 Cast Members for a Rollover Animation

2. Create another cast member of the same size but of a different color. This will be cast member 2.

3. Place the red cast member on the Stage. Select it. It should appear in sprite channel 1.

4. Choose Modify→Sprite→Script from the menu bar, and enter the following script.

```
on mouseEnter
    set the membernum of sprite 1 to 2
end

on mouseLeave
    set the membernum of sprite 1 to 1
end
```

This script switches the cast member assigned to this sprite from the red one (member 1) to the other one (member 2) when the mouse enters the sprite and then switches it back when the mouse leaves the sprite.

5. Try out your script by playing the movie and then rolling over the sprite with the mouse.

Creating MouseDown Animation

This works the same way as the rollover animation. Create two cast members of about the same size but different shapes, such as those shown in Figure 5.15.

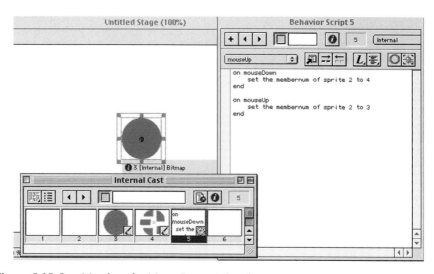

Figure 5.15 Cast Members for MouseDown Animation

Put the first cast member onto the Stage, and attach the following script to it.

```
on mouseDown
    set the membernum of sprite 2 to 4
end

on mouseUp
    set the membernum of sprite 2 to 3
end
```

This script works just like the rollover script but is triggered by a different event—the mouseDown event. Try it; you should see the round button appear to explode into pieces when you click on it.

☆ TIP   Events

Shockwave is a time- and event-based system—as a Shockwave project plays, it is always trying to move ahead the next frame and is keeping track of the events that occur. Along the way, certain events occur, some initiated by the user, others by the internal workings of the project. For instance, when the user clicks the mouse, two events occur: a mouseDown and a mouseUp. When Shockwave tries to leave the frame it's in and go to the next frame, an exitframe event occurs. These events can be picked up by scripts, such as the ones you just wrote, and used to trigger other events.

☆ SHORTCUT   Built-in Rollover Animations

You can also create a rollover animation with a built-in behavior. Create both sprites, place one on the Stage, and then open the Library palette. Under Animations, choose Interactive, and then choose Rollover Member Change. Drag this behavior from the Library palette onto the sprite on the Stage. Enter the cast number of the second sprite, and Shockwave will write your script for you.

Creating Moveable Sprites

To create a sprite that users can move, first put a cast member on the Stage, and then open its Property Inspector. In the Property Inspector, select the moveable sprite icon, as shown in Figure 5.16.

You can make any type of sprite moveable, but most often small sprites that represent objects or characters are given this treatment. Create a moveable sprite, play the movie, and then click and drag the sprite around the Stage. In later chapters, you will learn how to use moveable sprites to create some interesting types of interactivity.

☆ WARNING   Moveable ≠ Animated

A sprite cannot be at the same time animated along a path and moveable by the user. One or the other—Shockwave or the user—must be in control, not both at the same time.

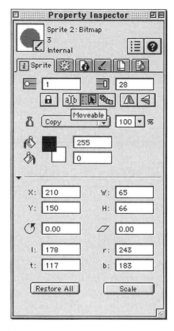

Figure 5.16 Making a Sprite Moveable

Looking Ahead

You have learned how to make your actors move around the Stage at your command or at the user's discretion. You have also learned how to make them move their body parts and speak. These capabilities alone can make a useful Shockwave project. But for a truly interactive production, you need to learn about scripts and logic. So on to the next chapters.

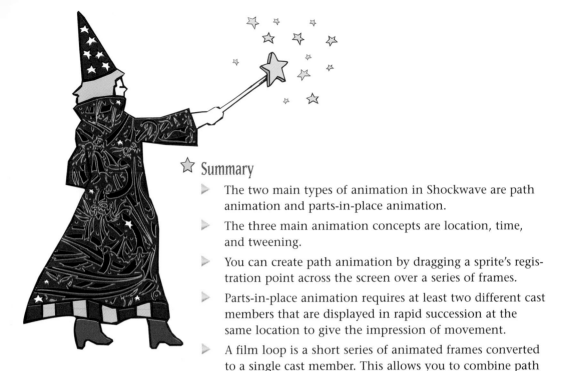

☆ Summary

▷ The two main types of animation in Shockwave are path animation and parts-in-place animation.

▷ The three main animation concepts are location, time, and tweening.

▷ You can create path animation by dragging a sprite's registration point across the screen over a series of frames.

▷ Parts-in-place animation requires at least two different cast members that are displayed in rapid succession at the same location to give the impression of movement.

▷ A film loop is a short series of animated frames converted to a single cast member. This allows you to combine path animation and parts-in-place animation.

▷ It's easy to set up an animation that users can initiate.

▷ Director provides built-in, prescripted animation behaviors you can use in Shockwave projects.

▷ Following guidelines for animation will make your Shockwave projects look and work better.

▷ You can write simple scripts to create rollover and mouseDown animations and to make moveable sprites.

☆ Online References

Sample Shockwave animations
`http://www.shockwave.com`

Cold Spring Harbor Laboratory Biology Animation Library—good examples of Shockwave animation for education and science
`http://www.dnalc.org/Shockwave/pcranwhole.html`

How Web Animation Works
`http://www.howstuffworks.com/web-animation.htm`

Radical Media Shockwave Showcase—interesting approach to Shockwave animation
`http://www.radicalmedia.com/~shockwave/index.html`

Tutorial on basic animation in Director
`http://www.macromedia.com/software/director/productinfo/tutorials/gettingstarted/`

Macromedia Director Support Center: Animation
`http://www.macromedia.com/support/director/animation.html`

Animation with Director and Shockwave
`http://www.utoronto.ca/atrc/education/workshops/web_express/`
`tutorials/director.html`

Tutorial: Animating Objects Along a Path
`http://www.fbe.unsw.edu.au/Learning/Director/animation/`
`tut1.htm`

☆ Review Questions

1. Explain the difference between path animation and parts-in-place animation, and describe when each might be used.

2. Describe the process of creating a simple path animation.

3. Describe the process of creating a simple parts-in-place animation.

4. Why and how would you create a film loop in a Shockwave project?

5. What are the advantages and disadvantages of using Director's built-in behaviors?

6. How many cast members do you need for a rollover animation? For a mouseDown animation?

7. Name some guidelines for creating effective animations.

☆ Hands-On Exercises

1. Create a simple path animation with a single sprite moving across the screen in a straight line. Then modify the path so that the sprite moves in a curve.

2. Recreate the animation in Exercise 1 so that the sprite begins full-size but ends up much smaller at the end of the animation.

3. Create a simple parts-in-place animation, like the example of the bird flapping its wings in this chapter. Then convert this animation to a film loop. Finally, animate the film loop along a path across the Stage.

4. Arrange your animation in the Score as described in this chapter to create an animation initiated by the user.

5. Create a sprite on the Stage and assign a built-in animation behavior to it.

6. Create a rollover or mouseDown animation.

7. Create a moveable sprite.

8. In your own Shockwave project, build at least two different kinds of animation, using your own content.

CHAPTER SIX

BUILDING BASIC INTERACTION

What a piece of work is man! . . .
in form and moving how express and admirable!
in action how like an angel!
—from *Hamlet*

The players are all rehearsed and on the stage waiting for the play to begin. They know how to move around the stage, and the audience is anxious for the show to begin. This chapter teaches you how to program the interaction of your Shockwave project, to get the cast members working with the user and with each other. You'll learn about *scripts* in this chapter—how they work, why you need them, and how to write them. And you'll write some scripts for your own project that enable you to build simple interactions.

◉◉ Chapter Objectives

☆ To understand how scripts work, why you need them, and how they are structured with the Lingo scripting language

☆ To learn how to write navigation scripts for a Shockwave project

☆ To learn how to control transitions with scripts

☆ To learn how to use scripts to control tempo

☆ To understand how to write scripts that perform if . . . then logic

☆ To examine some basic scripts that control sprites

☆ To learn how to create moveable sprites with drag-and-drop capability

☆ To bring these techniques together in your own Shockwave project

◎◎ How Scripts Work

As you develop the operational prototype of your own Shockwave project, you will need to use scripts to make it interactive. You have learned a few useful scripts already; this chapter explains the overall nature of scripts in Director and tells you how to write them.

Why Do I Need Scripts?

You need a script to do things that the Score cannot. The Score alone, without any scripts, can place items on the screen and make them move around. But to add interactivity, where the actions of the user control what happens, you need to use scripts. Without scripts, Director is simply an animation program. With scripts, you can design and program just about any kind of user interaction you want.

How Do Scripts Work?

Scripts wait for an event to take place (such as a mouse click or the movement of a sprite) and then trigger something else to happen. Take this script, for example:

```
on mouseUp
    go to "next part"
end
```

The event that the script waits for is a click of the mouse—a mouseUp event. As soon as it senses that event, it sends the program to the marker "next part".

Most scripts have this same structure:

```
on <some event>
   <do something>
   <do something else>
end
```

The list of <do something> lines can be as long as you wish, but they must be written in a language that the computer can understand. In Director, this language is called **Lingo**.

☆**TIP**   Lingo Syntax

Director allows two kinds of syntax with Lingo: the traditional "plain English" syntax you have seen so far and the newer "dot command" syntax. Shockwave projects work with either kind of syntax. Since the traditional syntax is easier for the novice to understand and compose, we use that form in this book.

Where Do I Write My Scripts?

Every script is attached to an object in Director. You can attach a script to four basic types of objects.

1. *A sprite that is on the Stage and in the Score.* Such a script will apply to anything that happens to that sprite while it is on the Stage in that frame. To write a script like this, select the sprite in the Score or on the Stage. Then choose Modify→Sprite→Script from the menu bar. This opens a Script window. Write your script in this window.

2. *A cast member.* Such a script will apply to that cast member, no matter where in the Score it appears. To attach a script to a cast member, select the cast member in the Cast window, and then click the script icon in the Cast window to get a Cast Script window. Enter your script here.

3. *The script channel in the Score.* Such a script will apply whenever this frame plays. To write one, double-click on the frame in the script channel where you want the script to appear, and you'll get a Script window.

4. *The entire movie.* This is called a movie script. Such a script applies to the entire movie. To write a movie script, open the Script window, and then in the Property Inspector select Movie from the Type pop-up menu.

Every object in your Director program can have its own script. When the user clicks the mouse, Director looks to see what object she clicked. If she clicked on a sprite, Director looks to see if that sprite has a script containing the on mouseUp event handler. (An **event handler** reacts to an event that happens as the movie is running.) If it does, then Director takes whatever action the script calls for. If Director does not find on mouseUp in the sprite script, it goes on to look in the script of the cast member. Should it find an on mouseUp event handler there, it will take the appropriate action. If it finds no on mouseUp event handler in the cast script, it goes on to look in the script channel for the frame that is currently running and acts accordingly. If it doesn't find on mouseUp there, it goes on to look for a movie script that contains on mouseUp. If it exhausts all possibilities and finds no script for responding to the mouseUp event, Director rests and does nothing. All this happens in a split second.

☆**WARNING**   The Hierarchy of Scripts

An event, such as a mouseUp, will be handled by the first script that it encounters, beginning with the sprite script, then moving to the cast member script, then to the script channel, and finally to the movie script.

What Can Scripts Do?

Scripts can make things happen. They can cause the program to jump to another marker. They can make a sound play. They can change the color or location of sprites on the Stage. They can save information for later use. They can test to see if a certain condition exists and then act accordingly. They can switch cast members in the Score. A script can make just about anything happen that the computer is capable of doing.

How Do I Find the Script to Do What I Want?

The Lingo language has hundreds of words that can make things happen. There is no way you can memorize them all. Most are similar to plain English, but all must be expressed in a very particular *syntax* for them to work. When you want to write a script but don't know what the exact words are, you can use the built-in Lingo dictionary. The steps below tell you what to do.

1. Open the Script window for the object to which you want to attach the script, and click your mouse in it.

2. Click the Lingo icon—a big letter L—in the Script window. See the long list of letters, with their accompanying terms, as shown in Figure 6.1.

3. Choose the term you think will cause the action you want. (For example, if you were trying to play a sound, you would look under So to Sq.)

4. When you have made your choice, a sample script will appear in your Script window, such as the following:

   ```
   sound playfile whichChannel, whichFile
   ```

5. Replace the placeholder words with the actual names and numbers of the objects to which you are referring. (Replace `whichChannel` with the number of the channel you want the sound to play in, and `whichFile` with the name of the sound file you want to play, so that your script reads

   ```
   sound playfile 1, "funnysound".)
   ```

   You have been using the alphabetic Lingo dictionary. Also in the Script window is a categorical Lingo dictionary, accessible by clicking the outline button next to the L icon.

   If the Lingo dictionaries do not yield a script that works for you, use the Director Help files. Open the Script window as before, then follow the steps below.

1. Choose Help→Lingo Dictionary from the menu bar.

2. Search this more explanatory dictionary alphabetically, by topic, or with a keyword search.

3. Read the explanation of exactly how the script should be written and what it does.

4. Copy the sample script if it seems relevant.

5. Go back to the Script window and paste in or write your script.

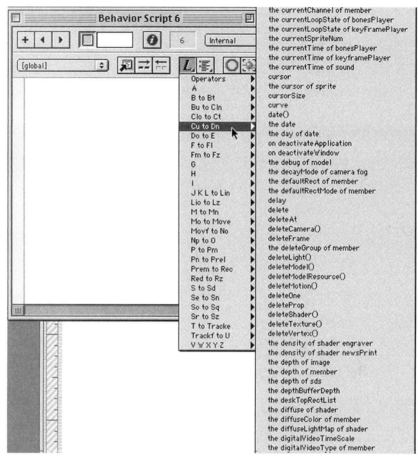

Figure 6.1 Using the Lingo Dictionary

As you write your own scripts and test them in your Shockwave projects, you will develop the skill of composing your own Lingo statements from scratch.

How Do I Use the Behavior Inspector?

You can also create a script by using the Behavior Inspector. Here's how.

1. Select the frame, sprite, or cast member to which you want to assign a script.

2. Open the Behavior Inspector.

3. Click the topmost + button.

4. Choose New Behavior from the pop-up menu.

5. Enter a name for this behavior. This is for your own reference.

6. Click the + button next to Events.

7. Choose the handler for the event to which you want the script to react.

8. Click the + button next to Action.

9. Select the action that you want to happen on that event.

10. Close the Behavior Inspector to compile the script.

You can see the script created by the Behavior Inspector by opening the Script window for the selected object.

☆ **SHORTCUT Watch the Colors of the Words**

As you write your scripts, pay attention to the colors of the words. Lingo handlers and commands appear in green. Acceptable connecting words appear in blue. Words not acceptable to Lingo appear in black. Words in quotes appear in gray. These colors help you see whether your script is acceptable.

How Do I Know If My Script Works?

When you close the Script window, Director compiles the script into computer code. As it does, it checks to see if the syntax of the script is correct. If it's not, Director will give you a message showing you what it didn't understand. Fix the script by checking with the various Lingo dictionaries or by examining the examples in this book.

Once you have an acceptable script, the only way to test it is to play the movie and try it. You need not run the entire project, just the part where your script occurs.

◎◎ Writing Navigation Scripts

A simple and necessary interactive function for your Shockwave project is navigation—enabling the user to get from one part of it to another. To build the basic interaction of "click and go," you need to write some navigation scripts.

To allow the user to navigate your Shockwave project, you will use devices such as menus, buttons, and clickable objects. Here are some ideas to get you started creating and scripting these navigation tools.

Creating Buttons for Navigation

To make a simple button that when clicked takes the user to a different part of the project, follow the steps below.

1. In the Tool Palette, select the button tool.

2. In the Stage, click and drag the rectangle of the button you wish to create. (The cursor will appear as a crosshair. Drag it across the place you want the button to appear.)

3. Enter some text for the button, such as "Go to Part 2."

4. Notice that this button has been added as a cast member in the Cast window.

5. To move the button, click its edge and drag it.

6. To stretch or shrink the button, drag from its corners.

7. To change its colors, select the text, and then use the foreground and background color chips in the Tool Palette to reset the colors of the text and the background.

   Now the button exists as a cast member and as a sprite. Next you need to script the button to do its work. To make a button into a navigation device, you must give it a script so that whenever the user clicks on the button, the script will be carried out. Here's how to add a script to a button.

8. Select the button on the Stage.

9. Choose Modify→Sprite→Script from the menu bar.

10. You will see the button's Script window. It should already be prescripted with `on mouseUp`, a blank line, and `end mouseUp`.

11. Into the blank line type your script. You might type something like one of the following:

    ```
    go to "somemarker"
    ```

    or

    ```
    play "somemarker"
    ```

12. Click the close box on the Script window, or click the lightning button. (The script is not compiled until you do this.)

13. Now your button has a script. The next time you click on the button while the movie is running, Director will carry out that script and go to the marker you named.

Creating Cast Members for Navigation

Any object on the Stage can be made into a navigation device: pictures, shapes, sprites, text, buttons, QuickTime movies, and so forth. To use a sprite for navigation, follow these steps.

1. On the Stage, select the sprite you want to make into a navigation device.

2. Open the sprite's Script window by choosing Modify→Sprite→Script from the menu bar.

3. Enter the desired script in the blank line between `on mouseUp` and `end`, such as `go to "somemarker"`.

4. Click the close box on the Script window. (The script is not compiled until you close its window.)

5. Now your sprite has a script. The next time you click on the sprite while the movie is running, Director will carry out that script.

Writing Navigation Scripts

Creating Text for Navigation

Words on the screen can become navigation devices, simply by creating a text cast member, putting it on the Stage, and then giving it a script. Here's how.

1. Create a text cast member. Use the Tool Palette, select the text tool (A), and drag the cursor across the Stage where you want the text to appear. Type the text into the box. The text is now a cast member, with a place in the Cast window.

2. To change size, font, or style, select the text, and then choose Modify→Font from the menu bar to make the changes.

3. To change the size of the text box, use the handle on its right side.

4. To change the position of the text box, click its edge and drag it.

5. Give the text sprite a script in the same way you assigned scripts to buttons and sprites above.

Creating Hot Areas on the Stage

You can make an area of the Stage sensitive to mouse clicks by creating a transparent sprite and giving it a script.

1. Use the Tool Palette to create a shape sprite on the Stage, with no color and no line, as shown in Figure 6.2.

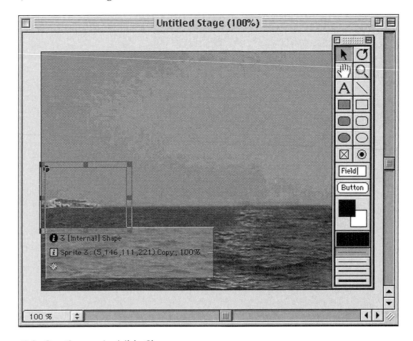

Figure 6.2 Creating an Invisible Shape

2. Place this invisible sprite over the place you want to be hot.

3. Assign this invisible sprite a script, following the instructions above.

Some Easy Lingo Scripts for Navigation

The following script will cause the program to jump to the marker you have named and continue playing from there. Don't forget the quotation marks!

```
on mouseUp
    go to "somemarker"
end mouseUp
```

The following script will cause the program to jump to the marker you have named and continue playing until it receives the command play done, at which point it jumps back to where it came from and continues playing.

```
on mouseUp
    play "somemarker"
end mouseUp
```

The following script will loop through the current frame over and over until another script sends the playhead elsewhere.

```
on exitframe
    go to the frame
end exitframe
```

Stopping the Forward Motion

To allow your users to click the navigation devices you have just created, you may need to stop the forward motion of the playhead through the frames. As you have already discovered, the Director program will keep going forward to the next frame unless you stop it. This is best done with a **go-to-the-frame loop**. Put this script in the script channel in the Score:

```
on exitFrame
    go to the frame
end
```

This will cause the program to repeat this frame over and over. Sound and QuickTime movies will continue to play, and all clickable and moveable sprites will be live. This is the most flexible option to use for stopping the forward motion of the program, since it allows you to trap many types of events by adding if . . . then lines to the script. The project in Figure 6.3 shows scripts in the script channel of some of its frames—these are go-to-the-frame scripts.

Setting Up Your Navigation

Armed with the knowledge of navigation scripting, set up your own Shockwave project with markers, sprites, and devices that let the user navigate from one part of the program to another. When you are finished, your Score should look something like Figure 6.3.

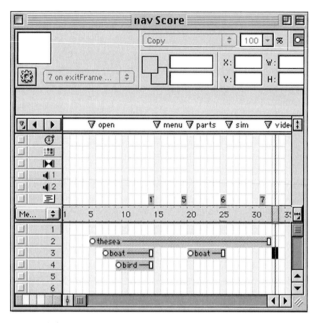

Figure 6.3 Score Setup for Navigation

◎◎ Controlling Transitions

You can create transitions in two ways in Director: as a *frame transition* placed in the transition channel of the Score, or as a *puppet transition* included in a Lingo script.

Frame Transitions

The transition channel in the Score is where you program in the fades, dissolves, and wipes that you want the user to see as the Shockwave project moves from one frame to the next. Double-click on a frame in the transition channel (it's just above the sound channel) to get a list of possible transitions. Notice that many of them are adjustable as to smoothness and duration.

When using transitions, it's easy to get carried away with visual effects. To avoid this, remember these two principles.

1. *Be consistent.* Try to stick with one type of transition throughout the project. It's easier on the eyes, more predictable, and less jarring.

2. *Use an appropriate transition.* When moving from left to right, as through the pages of a book, use simple wipes. Dissolves give a soft effect for artistic screens. To show tension, use strips and Venetian blinds.

Transitions take time, and they slow or stop the motion of sprites on the Stage. The playhead stops as the transition completes itself. So avoid using a frame transition in a sequence with ongoing animation.

☆**WARNING** **Don't Mix Transitions with Go-to-the-Frame Loops**

Do not put a transition in the transition channel in a frame with a go-to-the-frame loop. If you do, the transition will occur over and over every time Shockwave loops through the frame. You won't see the transition because nothing is changing, but it will be happening. You'll know it's happening because the cursor will disappear for the time it takes to do the transition. If you want to transition into a frame with a go-to-the-frame loop, use a puppet transition instead.

Puppet Transitions

You can issue a Lingo script to make a transition happen, as shown in the script below.

```
on mouseUp
    puppettransition 51, 4
    go to "mymarker"
end mouseUp
```

This will cause a one-second fast dissolve as the program moves into the frame `mymarker`. The first number (51) indicates the type of transition (for example, wipe right, dissolve, and so on); the second number indicates the length of the transition in quarters of a second. Each type of transition has a number, as indicated in Table 6.1.

Table 6.1 Puppet Transition Numbers and Their Descriptions

Number	Description	Number	Description
01	Wipe right	11	Push left
02	Wipe left	12	Push right
03	Wipe down	13	Push down
04	Wipe up	14	Push up
05	Center out, horizontal	15	Reveal up
06	Edges in, horizontal	16	Reveal up, right
07	Center out, vertical	17	Reveal right
08	Edges in, vertical	18	Reveal down, right
09	Center out, square	19	Reveal down
10	Edges in, square	20	Reveal down, left

(continues)

Table 6.1 Puppet Transition Numbers and Their Descriptions *(continued)*

Number	Description	Number	Description
21	Reveal left	37	Venetian blinds
22	Reveal up, left	38	Checkerboard
23	Dissolve, pixels, fast*	39	Strips on bottom, build left
24	Dissolve, boxy rectangles	40	Strips on bottom, build right
25	Dissolve, boxy squares	41	Strips on left, build down
26	Dissolve, patterns	42	Strips on left, build up
27	Random rows	43	Strips on right, build down
28	Random columns	44	Strips on right, build up
29	Cover down	45	Strips on top, build left
30	Cover down, left	46	Strips on top, build right
31	Cover down, right	47	Zoom open
32	Cover left	48	Zoom close
33	Cover right	49	Vertical blinds
34	Cover up	50	Dissolve, bits, fast*
35	Cover up, left	51	Dissolve, pixels*
36	Cover up, right	52	Dissolve, bits*

* These transitions do not work with monitors set to 32-bit color.

☆ **SHORTCUT Sprite Transitions from the Library Palette**

Another way to make a sprite appear with a visual transition is to drag a sprite transition from the Library palette to the sprite in the Score. Open the Library palette, choose Animations→Sprite Transitions, then drag and drop the desired transition on the sprite in the Score.

◎◎ Controlling Tempo

The tempo of a Director movie indicates how quickly it will move through the frames. The tempo is expressed in frames per second. Use the tempo channel in the Score to speed up or slow down the program. You have some options for how to do this.

☆ Change the frame playback rate.

☆ Insert a delay for a certain number of seconds.

☆ Wait for a sound or QuickTime movie to finish before going on.

These choices are available by double-clicking in a frame in the tempo channel. This opens a dialog box like the one shown in Figure 6.4.

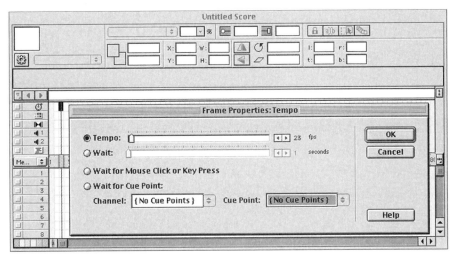

Figure 6.4 Programming the Tempo Channel

But remember that not all computers can play your movie at the tempo you set—-a project with lots of large animated sprites moving at once will slow down on all but the fastest computers. The movie will proceed at a frame rate lower than what you set.

◎◎ Using Conditional Tests (If . . . Then . . . Logic)

In many cases you will want Shockwave to check to see whether something has happened and then do something based on that action. For example, you could provide the user with a blank editable text field to type into, along with the question, "Which is the largest sail on this boat?" and a submit button. When the user clicks the button, a script will check to see if he or she entered the right answer. The script, attached to the button, appears below.

```
on mouseUp
   if field "typeithere" contains "mainsail" then
      go to "correct"
   else
      go to "incorrect"
   end if
end
```

"Correct" and "incorrect" are two different markers in the Score that display the appropriate feedback to the user.

Notice the structure of the if . . . then script. It contains three elements and a conclusion. The three elements are listed below.

1. The condition to be tested, for example, `field "typeithere" contains "mainsail"`.

   A condition is either true or false. If it's true, Shockwave performs whatever action comes right after the word `then` in the script. If it's false, Shockwave performs the command that comes after the `else` in the script. The word `contains` is a Lingo script word.

2. The "if true" command, for example, `go to "correct"`.

3. The "if false" command, for example, `go to "incorrect"`.

   If . . . then logic is essential to interactivity in Shockwave.

◎◎ Using Scripts for Sprite Control

Hiding or Showing a Sprite

You can cause a sprite on the Stage to become invisible or visible by controlling its visibility with a script. Suppose you want the bird (sprite 3) to disappear whenever the user clicks on it. To do this, attach a script to the bird such as the one shown below.

```
on mouseUp
   set the visible of sprite 3 to false
end mouseUp
```

A sprite channel remains invisible—even if another sprite is put into it—until that channel is made visible again. To bring the bird back again, create a button on the Stage that uses the following script.

```
on mouseUp
   set the visible of sprite 3 to true
end mouseUp
```

Changing the Location of a Sprite

Suppose you want the bird to move when the user clicks the boat. You can change the location of the bird by attaching to the boat a script like the one shown here.

```
on mouseUp
   set the locV of sprite 3 to 56
   set the locH of sprite 3 to 123
end
```

This will move the bird (sprite 3) to a location on the Stage that is 56 pixels across and 123 pixels down from the upper-left corner. The vertical location, `locV`, is measured from the top of the screen, while the horizontal location, `locH`, is measured from the left side of the screen. You can combine both the vertical and horizontal coordinates into a single statement such as `set the loc of sprite 3 to point(56,123)`.

Picking Up the Collision of Two Sprites

You will often animate or make moveable sprites on the Stage and want to keep track of whether they bump in to each other, so that you can initiate events based on their actions. Suppose you want to make the animated bird (sprite 3) disappear whenever it comes in contact with the animated boat (sprite 4). You could write a script in the script channel like the one below.

```
on exitframe
  if sprite 4 intersects 3 then
    set the visible of sprite 3 to false
  else
    set the visible of sprite 3 to true
  end if
  go to the frame
end
```

This script uses if . . . then logic to see whether the boat (sprite 4) intersects the bird (sprite 3). If they intersect, then the script makes the bird disappear. If the two sprites do not intersect, then the script makes the bird visible.

A similar script can tell whether one sprite is completely inside another by using the Lingo term `within`, as shown below.

```
on exitframe
  if sprite 4 within sprite 3 then
    set the visible of sprite 3 to false
  else
    set the visible of sprite 3 to true
  end if
  go to the frame
end
```

Figure 6.5 shows the difference between a sprite intersecting with and being within another sprite: on the left, the two sprites intersect; in the second pair, one sprite is within the other.

◎◎ Creating Drag-and-Drop Sprites

The manipulation of objects on the screen is an important method of building interactivity into a Shockwave project. This set of instructions shows how to let the user drag and drop sprites and to "snap" these sprites into place. Think of this as a form of manipulation, as if you are letting the audience grab and move the actors on the Stage.

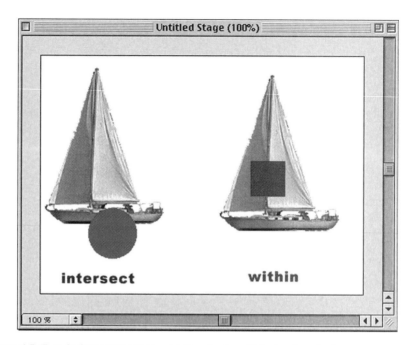

Figure 6.5 Two Sprites Intersecting and One Sprite within Another Sprite

Enabling Drag

You can make any sprite draggable by the user, so that when the user clicks on the sprite and then drags with the mouse button still down, the sprite will move along with the mouse. In Director, such a sprite is called a **moveable sprite**. You can make a sprite moveable by selecting it on the Stage, then selecting the Moveable box at the top of the Property Inspector window. You can also make a sprite moveable with a script such as the following.

```
on mouseUp
    set the moveableSprite of sprite 3 to true
end mouseUp
```

The user can drag the moveable sprite anywhere on the screen when the movie is running. You can make any type of sprite moveable: big or small, text, paint, shape, or video. In fact, you can make a big, giant sprite, bigger than the Stage, and make it moveable, to achieve effects such as a scrolling map or an aimable flashlight.

However, a sprite that is animated in the Score with a path animation cannot also be moveable. Either the user has control or the Score has control, but not both.

The first step in creating drag-and-drop interactivity is to create a sprite and make it moveable. Next you'll learn how to let the user drop the sprite to initiate an interaction.

Enabling Drop

After the user drags a sprite, he or she usually drops it somewhere by letting go of it. This is called a **drop**. The user drops a sprite by letting up on the mouse button, thus causing a mouseUp event to occur. By trapping this mouseUp event, you can cause your Shockwave project to respond to this act of dropping the sprite. Often you want something to happen depending on exactly where the user drops the sprite. Here's a script, attached to a moveable sprite, that will elicit a beep if the user drops the sprite in a certain place.

```
on mouseUp
   if sprite 3 within sprite 6 then beep
end mouseUp
```

In this script, if the user drops the moveable sprite (sprite 3) inside the boundaries of the target sprite (sprite 6), then the computer will beep.

Enabling Snap

Following a similar procedure, you can make the sprite snap back to where it was if the user drops it in the wrong place. Use a script such as the following.

```
on mouseUp
   if sprite 3 within sprite 6 then
     beep
   else
     puppetsound 1, "boing"
     set the loc of sprite 3 to point(100,200)
   end if
end mouseUp
```

How do you know the point coordinates to send the sprite back to? Take the following steps.

1. Put the sprite where you want it to snap back to.

2. In the Message window, type `put the loc of sprite` 3, then press return.

3. The Message window will respond with something like `point (100,200)`. This means that the location of sprite 3 is at a point 100 pixels across and 200 pixels down from the upper-left corner of the Stage. This is the point you want it to snap back to.

☆**TIP**   **The Message Window**

The Message window allows you to command and query Director without adding a script to your project. You write the script in the Message window, and Director carries it out immediately, even if the movie is not playing. This capability is useful for obtaining information about an object (for example, `put the forecolor of sprite 3`) or for making something happen (for example, `set the locH of sprite 5 to 435`).

By accompanying this snap with a sound that indicates failure (the "boing" in the script), you have made it clear to the user that he or she didn't drop the sprite in the right place.

A Drag-and-Drop Example

To illustrate a typical drag-and-drop interaction in a Shockwave project, let's go through the process of creating an exercise that lets the user identify the parts of a sailboat with a puzzle-like activity. The user will be asked to drag the various parts of the boat to their correct locations on a picture of the sea in the background. Here are the steps.

1. *Create the cast members.* In this example, we create six additional cast members, as shown in Figure 6.6.

   ✤ A picture of the hull

   ✤ A picture of the mainsail

   ✤ A picture of the jib

   ✤ A picture of the sea (background)

   ✤ A voice that says, "That's right!"

   ✤ A "boing" noise that indicates a wrong answer

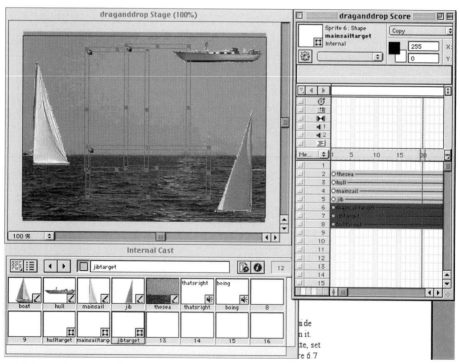

Figure 6.6 Cast Members and Targets for Drag-and-Drop Exercise

2. *Set up the targets.* The targets in this example will be invisible rectangles that indicate the correct placement of the parts of the boat. We create three target rectangles, one for each part, as shown in Figure 6.6.

These targets must be larger in all dimensions than the cast members that will go inside them—each at least 10 pixels taller and wider than the sprite that will be dropped on it. To create an invisible rectangle, select the unfilled rectangle tool from the Tool Palette, set the line width to zero, then click and drag on the Stage in the appropriate spot. Figure 6.7 shows these tools in the Tool Palette.

☆**TIP   Moving One Sprite at a Time**

You may end up with overlapping sprites as you develop this drag-and-drop example, which are difficult to select and move. Try selecting in the Score the sprite you want to move, and then use the arrows on the keyboard to move it on the Stage.

3. *Place the cast members on the Stage.* Next we drag the boat parts from the Cast window to the Stage, placing them around the edge in what are obviously incorrect locations, as shown in Figure 6.6.

4. *Make the sprites moveable.* Next we select each of the boat parts in turn and use the Property Inspector to make them moveable by clicking the Moveable button.

5. *Script the sprites.* We then write a script on each sprite that tells the user she or he is correct if the sprite drops within the target. Here's an example of such a script.

Figure 6.7 Tools for Creating an Invisible Rectangle

```
on mouseUp
    if sprite 2 within sprite 5
    then
        puppetsound 1, "That's right!"
    else
        set the loc of sprite 2 to point (25,34)
        puppetsound 1, "boing"
    end if
end mouseUp
```

In this script, sprite 2 is the hull, sprite 5 is the hull target rectangle, and (25,34) is the original location of the hull sprite. If the user drops the hull within its target, she or he will hear "That's right!", and the hull will stay where it was dropped. Otherwise, the user will hear the "boing" sound and see the hull snap back to where it started. We add the same script, with different sprite numbers, to the mainsail and jib sprites.

6. *Test the exercise.* Finally, we play the movie and try placing the boat pieces as a user would. If necessary, we correct the scripts.

Follow these same steps to create a drag-and-drop exercise for your own Shockwave project.

◎◎ Trying It Yourself

The best way to consolidate your learning of all these methods for creating interactivity is to build them into your own Shockwave project. Try the following suggestions.

☆ Create several scenes, each with a marker and a go-to-the-frame loop.

☆ Create several devices that allow the user to navigate from scene to scene, such as "click and go" buttons.

☆ Create some transitions from scene to scene.

☆ Allow the user to make a sprite disappear.

☆ Allow the user to change the location of a sprite by clicking on a different sprite.

☆ Create a sprite that the user can move.

☆ Detect a collision of two sprites.

☆ Arrange and script a drag-and-drop exercise that includes if . . . then logic.

As you add these forms of interactivity, your production will seem to have a life of its own. The actors in your play not only appear, move, and speak—they now also respond to the user's actions. The next chapter will take this interactivity further, allowing the user to take more control of what happens in your project.

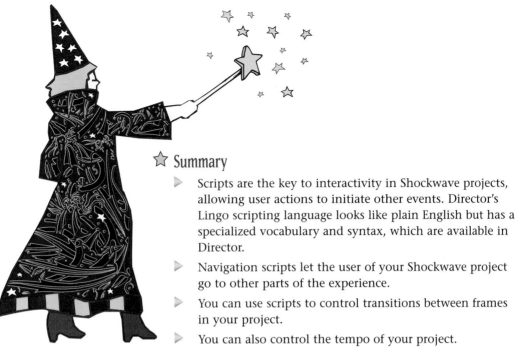

☆ Summary

▷ Scripts are the key to interactivity in Shockwave projects, allowing user actions to initiate other events. Director's Lingo scripting language looks like plain English but has a specialized vocabulary and syntax, which are available in Director.

▷ Navigation scripts let the user of your Shockwave project go to other parts of the experience.

▷ You can use scripts to control transitions between frames in your project.

▷ You can also control the tempo of your project.

▷ If . . . then logic is a key component of scripting for interactivity.

▷ Simple scripts allow you to control the visibility and location of sprites and to determine when two sprites collide.

▷ Drag-and-drop experiences enable the user to manipulate elements of your Shockwave project on the screen.

▷ Experimenting within your own Shockwave project is the best way to learn how to create interactivity.

☆ Online References

An introduction to Lingo scripting
`http://www.cs.vu.nl/~eliens/onderwijs/multimedia/imm/college/@archive/director/scripting.html`

Tips for scripting in Lingo
`http://www.mcli.dist.maricopa.edu/director/tips-script.html`

How to write a simple script
`http://www.fbe.unsw.edu.au/Learning/Director/Scripting/tut13.htm`

How to use Director 8 behaviors
`http://www.macromedia.com/support/director/lingo/d8/d8behaviors.html`

☆ Review Questions

1. Describe the basic structure of a simple Lingo script.

2. Why are scripts necessary to a Shockwave project?

3. List at least two kinds of scripts used for navigation.

4. Explain the role of a go-to-the-frame script in a Shockwave project.

5. How can scripts make a sprite move or make it appear and disappear?

6. Describe how to script if . . . then logic and how you might use it in a Shockwave project.

7. Explain how you can change the tempo of a Shockwave movie.

8. Why might you use a drag-and-drop exercise in a Shockwave project? How is it constructed?

☆ Hands-On Exercises

1. In your own Shockwave project, create a button that when clicked takes the user to another marker. Do the same with a text cast member and with a paint cast member.

2. In the first frame of one of the scenes in your Shockwave project, insert a transition using the transitions channel in the Score. Compare the results with other types of transitions. Now create the same transition with a Lingo script.

3. Write a script that performs the following actions.

   a. Makes a sprite invisible
   b. Makes a sprite visible
   c. Moves a sprite around the Stage

4. Write an if . . . then script in your project that tests to see if a condition is true and performs some action as a result.

5. Write a script that detects the collision of two sprites.

6. Develop a simple exercise in your Shockwave project that involves drag, drop, and snap, as described in this chapter.

CHAPTER SEVEN

CREATING COMPLEX INTERACTION

When sorrows come, they come not single spies,
but in battalions.

—from *Hamlet*

This chapter takes you farther down the road of interactivity, showing you how to use Lingo scripts to
build animation that is responsive to the user's
actions, to control and modify sprites in real time, to create
sliders and other devices that let the user control the
Shockwave environment, and to make text interactive in a
variety of ways. Along the road, you'll also learn how to build
randomness into your project and to use repeat loops. There's
a battalion of techniques in this chapter to help you build
more complex interactions; by combining them into your
own project there's no limit to the possibilities.

Chapter Objectives

☆ To learn how to animate a sprite with a Lingo script
and how to program random events into a Shockwave
project

☆ To learn how to modify sprites with Lingo scripts and how to build sliders that enable the user to modify the Shockwave environment

☆ To learn how to use scripts to make text interactive

☆ To learn how to make sound interactive

☆ To learn how to make video interactive

☆ To learn how to interact with Web resources

☆ To learn how to create custom cursors

☆ To learn how to write a script for score keeping

◎◎ Animating with Lingo Scripts

By using the various location commands in Lingo, you can use scripts to move sprites around on the Stage. Let's look at a simple sprite script.

```
on mouseUp
   set the loc of sprite 3 to point(200,100)
end mouseUp
```

This script moves the sprite from wherever it was to a point 200 pixels across and 100 pixels down from the upper-left corner of the Stage. But this movement will be abrupt and unnatural. To make the sprite move smoothly around the screen, you need to increment the changes in location a few pixels at a time.

Here is another frame script. When placed in a go-to-the-frame loop, it moves the sprite across the Stage horizontally from left to right.

```
on exitframe
   set the locH of sprite 3 to (the locH of sprite 3) + 5
   go to the frame
end exitframe
```

Each time Shockwave loops through this frame, the sprite moves 5 pixels to the right. Played at 30 frames per second, it takes the sprite about 5 seconds to move across a 750-pixel wide Stage, in a nice smooth movement.

☆**WARNING** Moving Off the Stage

The script above, if left to play over and over, will eventually move the sprite to a location off the Stage, where the user will not be able to see it and you, the developer, will lose track of it. So be careful when incrementing sprite locations in continuous loops, or include a command such as `if the locH of sprite 3 > 750 then exit`.

☆ **TIP**   **Increments**

You can use this incrementing function in many ways in Lingo scripts. A script like this sets the new value (in this case, the sprite's horizontal location) by looking at the current value and adding a small number to it. So if the sprite's location was 150 pixels across the Stage, this script moves it to 155 pixels. In the same way, you can increment the score of a game, the height of a sprite, the volume of a sound, or the blend of a sprite.

Scripting Random Movement

The sprite scripted above will move in a predictable, straight line across the Stage. But suppose the sprite were an ant walking on the sidewalk. Ants seldom move in straight lines, and to us their movement seems random: a little to the left, a little to the right, back and forth. You can use Lingo scripts to create this kind of unpredictable movement. Such a frame script might look like the one shown below.

```
on exitframe
    Set the locH of sprite 3 to (the locH of sprite 3) +
        random(6) -3
    Set the locV of sprite 3 to (the locV of sprite 3) +
        random(6) -3
    go to the frame
end
```

The net result of this script is to add a random number between –2 and 3 to the location of the sprite each time Shockwave loops through the frame. That's because the function `random(6)` generates a random number between 1 and 6 each time it is called. By subtracting 3 from each of these values, we end up with numbers ranging from –2 (1 minus 3) to 3 (6 minus 3). Since the number is unpredictable at each loop, we see the sprite move at random on the Stage. By adjusting these numbers slightly, you can make the sprite move in bigger steps or make it slowly move in one direction or another, but in a random way.

You can also use scripts like these to increment other attributes of the sprite, such as rotation, height, width, blend, and color, in linear as well as random patterns. Some of these, along with their Lingo vocabulary and possible values, are shown in Table 7.1.

Table 7.1 Some Sprite Properties to Set with Lingo

Attribute	Lingo Syntax	Units	Values
Horizontal location	`locH` `locV`	Pixels	No limit, but all negative values and values greater than the width of the Stage will place the sprite off the Stage and out of view.
Vertical location	`set the locH of sprite 3 to 500`		
Rotation	`rotation` `set the rotation of sprite 3 to 45`	Degrees	360 degrees is one complete clockwise rotation; –720 degrees would be two complete turns counterclockwise.
Blend	`blend` `set the blend of sprite 3 to 55`	Percent of opacity	0 to 100 scale: 0 is transparent, 100 is opaque.
Color	`forecolor` `backcolor` `set the forecolor of sprite 3 to 125`	RGB color numbers	White is 0, black is 32767; other colors are numbers in between.
Height	`height` `width` `set the height of sprite 3 to 56`	Pixels	Positive numbers only are used for these attributes.
Width			

Scripting Other Random Events

Suppose you want the bird you have seen in previous examples to sing at odd intervals. You can do this with a script that uses the `random()` function. Here is a script to put in the script channel that causes the bird to sing at random, on the average of once every 20 cycles of the go-to-the-frame loop.

```
on exitframe
    if random(20) = 1 then puppetsound 1, "birdsong"
    go to the frame
end
```

This assumes you have a sound called `birdsong` in the Cast window. Each time the movie loops through this frame, the computer generates a random number from 1 to 20. If this number equals 1, the program plays the bird song in channel 1. If the computer generates a number other than 1, nothing happens. So on average, 1 time out of 20 the bird will sing.

You can also use this function to make other events happen randomly. Try a script like the one below in the script channel.

```
on exitframe
   if random(20) = 1 then play "<marker>"
   go to the frame
end
```

◎◎ Controlling and Modifying Sprites with Scripts

Switching Cast Members

In Chapter Five you learned how to make rollover and mouseDown scripts that changed the appearance of a sprite by switching in a new cast member. Switching cast members is a useful function that is easy to accomplish with a Lingo script. The basic command for this takes the form `set the member of sprite 3 to "membername"`. You can also refer to the replacement cast member by its number, as in `set the membernum of sprite 3 to 5`. The new cast member will replace the old at the same sprite location on the Stage and will also take its place in the Score.

Figure 7.1 shows an example of how you might use this switching of cast members. When the user drags and drops the flying bird onto the nest, it switches to a sitting bird.

To build this example, you first create two birds, one flying (cast member 1, `flybird`) and one sitting (cast member 4, `sitbird`). (The flying bird could be a film loop if you like.) You'll also need a nest, bigger than the bird, to drop the bird into. Place the nest onto the Stage as sprite 4 and the flying bird as sprite 5. Make the flying bird into a moveable sprite. Create a go-to-the-frame loop in the script channel.

Attach the following script to the flying bird.

```
on mouseUp
   if sprite 5 within 4 then
      set the member of sprite 5 to "sitbird"
   else
      set the member of sprite 5 to "flybird"
   end if
end mouseUp
```

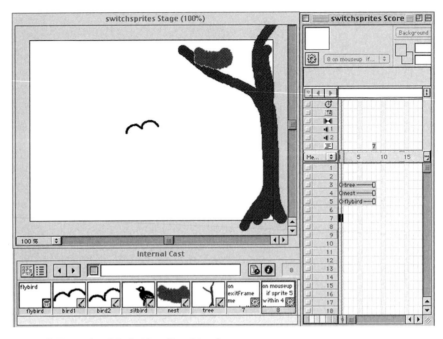

Figure 7.1 Example of Switching Cast Members

Run the movie, drag and drop the bird on the nest, and see what happens. If the flying bird is within the nest, you will see the flying bird switch to the sitting bird. If you drag and drop it outside the nest, it will change back to the flying bird.

Dealing with Visibility

If you use a script to make a sprite invisible, you will find that its sprite channel remains invisible—even in other scenes much later in the Score—until you make it visible again. This can cause problems; for example, if you forget that sprite 6 is invisible and you place a sprite in that channel later in the project, you won't be able to see it. So if you use invisibility at all, it's a good idea to make all sprites visible when you begin a new scene. This is easy to do with a script placed in the first frame of the new scene, in the script channel, right under the marker.

```
on exitframe
    set the visible of sprite 3 to true
end
```

If you wanted to make all the channels you are using visible, you could simply expand this script with additional lines.

```
on exitframe
   set the visible of sprite 1 to true
   set the visible of sprite 2 to true
   set the visible of sprite 3 to true
   set the visible of sprite 4 to true
   set the visible of sprite 5 to true
   (and so forth)
end
```

Using Repeat Loops

A repeat loop can make a script perform an action over and over. For example, if you are making a long series of sprite channels visible as in the script above, this scripting can get tedious. Using a repeat loop and a variable can make this and other such processes more efficient. A script to make sprite channels 1 through 15 visible would look like the one below.

```
on exitframe
   repeat with x = 1 to 15
      set the visible of sprite x to true
   end repeat
end exitframe
```

In this script, x is a variable that takes on a different value each time the loop repeats. In the first iteration, x equals 1, and sprite 1 is made visible. In the second iteration, x equals 2, and sprite 2 becomes visible, and so forth until x equals 15.

You can use repeat loops with variables for other interactive purposes, such as searching long fields full of text. Below is a script that searches for a key word in a long text passage and highlights it if found. The key word is entered into a user-editable text field called `searchword`. The text passage is in a field called `textpassage`.

```
on mouseUp
   repeat with x = 1 to the number of words of field
         "textpassage"
      if word x of field "textpassage" contains field
            "searchword" then
         hilite word x of field "textpassage"
      end if
   end repeat
end mouseUp
```

This script causes Shockwave to look at each word in the text passage in turn to see if it contains the search word. If it does, Shockwave highlights (selects) the word. If it doesn't, the repeat loop proceeds to the next word.

Using Sliders to Control the Environment

An interactive way to let the user adjust things in the Shockwave environment is to provide a slider. The user slides a little sprite up and down (or across) a fixed line, and by doing so causes something else to change in value. For instance, you might include a volume control slider in your project. You would do this by creating a frame where music is playing continuously in sound channel 1. Then you'd create a slider that turns the volume of this sound up and down.

A slider consists of two sprites: a line and a slider. The slider moves along the line, and as it is moved, it causes a value to change, depending on where it is on the line. Here are step-by-step instructions for creating a simple slider that controls the volume of a sound.

1. Place a long musical sound in sound channel 1 of the Score.

2. Place a go-to-the-frame script in the script channel at the last frame of the music.

3. Create a line sprite and a slider sprite, like those shown in Figure 7.2, and place them on the Stage in the same frame as the go-to-the-frame loop.

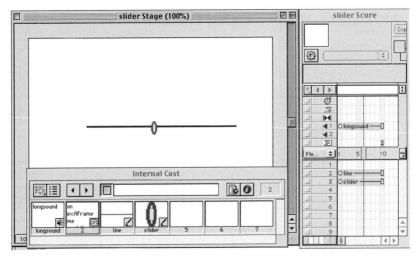

Figure 7.2 Making a Slider

4. Make the line sprite exactly 255 pixels wide, and place it on the Stage so its locH is 100, as shown in Figure 7.2. Put it in sprite channel 2.

5. Make the slider a moveable sprite. Put it in sprite channel 3.

6. Modify part of the go-to-the-frame script in the script channel to read:

```
on exitFrame
    set the constraint of sprite 3 to 2
        set the volume of sound 1 to (the locH of
            sprite 3) - 100
    go to the frame
end
```

7. Play the movie, hear the sound, and move the slider to adjust the volume.

When the user drags the slider and releases the mouse, the script sets the volume of the sound to a new value based on the slider's position. If the slider is at locH 100, the volume is zero. If the slider is at locH 200, the volume is midrange, and with the slider at locH 355, the user hears the sound at full volume.

A slider of similar structure could also modify

☆ The rotation of a sprite

☆ The blend of a sprite

☆ The width or height of a sprite

☆ The color of a sprite

☆ The location of a sprite

☆ The amount of randomness in a sprite's movement

☆ The text size of a word

☆ The next frame to visit

☆ The tempo of the Shockwave movie

☆ The playback rate of a QuickTime video

☆ Any other parameter that can be expressed as a number

You may have to perform a little mathematical calculation on the numbers in the script to match the range of the parameter you are setting. The script above adjusts volume from 0 to 255. To adjust the blend of a sprite, you'd have to make the line shorter or divide the result by 2.5, since the values for blend range from 0 (invisible) to 100 (opaque). It's much easier to work with sliders if you set the length of the line to be exactly as long (in pixels) as the range of possible values of the parameter you're adjusting.

Using this same method, you could use the script line below for a slider that controls a number displayed in a field, as shown in Figure 7.3.

```
put the locH of sprite 3 into field "indicator"
```

In this case the number that represents the horizontal location of the slider is displayed in a text field on the Stage. For this to work continuously, the script should be placed in the script channel in a go-to-the-frame loop.

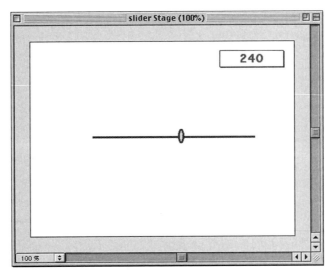

Figure 7.3 A Slider That Controls a Number Displayed in a Field

◎◎ Enabling Text Functions with Lingo

You can change and search field text (but not bitmapped or rich text) with Lingo scripts. For instance, a script like the one below changes the style of a word in a text field.

```
on mouseUp
  set the fontstyle of word 4 of field "mytextfield" to "bold"
end mouseUp
```

In similar fashion, you can change the color, size, and font of the text, using Lingo commands such as those listed below.

```
set the forecolor of word 5 of field "mytextfield" to 125
set the fontsize of word 5 of field "mytextfield" to 36
set the font of field "mytextfield" to "Times"
```

You can also add and subtract words from a text field, using scripts such as this one.

```
put "Here is the new text. " into field "mytextfield"
```

This replaces whatever is already in the field with the new string of words.

A script such as the one below does not replace what's already in the text field but adds the new text onto the end.

```
put "I am adding more text." after field "mytextfield"
```

After running the last five scripts, the text field would look like the one shown in Figure 7.4.

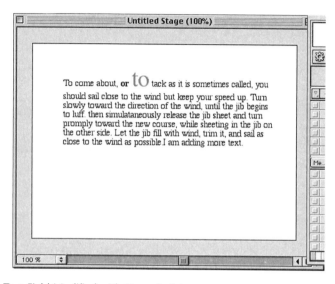

Figure 7.4 Text Field Modified with Lingo Scripts

Creating Hypertext Systems

Director can tell which word a user clicked in a text field (but not in rich text or bitmapped text). A script like the one below, attached to the text field, tells you which word was clicked.

```
on mouseUp
    put the mouseword into field 4
end mouseUp
```

Extending this logic a bit, you can make your Shockwave program do various things depending on which word the user clicks. Attach a script like this one to a text field.

```
on mouseUp
    if word (the mouseword) of field 1 = "hello" then beep
end mouseUp
```

This causes a beep only if the user clicks on the word "hello" in the text field. Another way to use this kind of script is to jump to another marker if the user clicks a certain word.

```
on mouseUp
    if word (the mouseword) of field 1 = "cat" then go to "cat"
end mouseUp
```

An easy way to make speaking text is to have each word recorded as a separate sound cast member with its name the same as the word. Then use a script like this to play the sounds as the user clicks the words.

```
on mouseUp
    puppetsound 1,(word (the mouseword) of field 1)
end mouseUp
```

A similar script can create pop-up definitions for words in a text field. Write the text passage in text field 1. Then create each definition as a text cast member, and assign it a name the same as the word it defines. For instance, the cast member named "cat" is a text member containing "A feline animal with four legs and nine lives." In the following script, sprite 6 is a definition box into which different cast members are placed depending on which word is clicked.

```
on mouseUp
    set the member of sprite 6 to member (word (the mouseword) of
        field 1)
end mouseUp
```

When the user clicks a word in field 1, this script puts into sprite channel 6 the cast member whose name is the word that was clicked.

Creating String Functions

Text on a computer is often referred to as **string data** because words and sentences are like strings of characters arranged one after another with no internal logic, unlike numbers, where the order of the characters is critical and the entire number represents a unique ordered value. Lingo provides several ways of working with strings, including the `mouseword` function used in the scripts above, as well as others.

In a text field, `the mouseline` indicates the number of the line of text that the user clicked. A line is the string of words between return characters, not the actual lines displayed in the field. For instance, the text field shown in Figure 7.5 contains five lines. This function returns a number, not a line of text. To refer to the text contained in the line, you would use a script like `line (the mouseline) of field "mytextfield"`.

In a text field, `the mouseword` indicates the number of the word that the user clicked. A word is the string of characters between spaces. This function returns a number; to refer to the word you would use a script like `word (the mouseword) of field "mytextfield"`.

The Lingo term `char` (short for characters) refers to an individual letter of a word. So in Figure 7.5 above, `char 1 of word 2 of field "mytextfield"` would refer to "r". Lines, words, and characters are called

chunks of text in the Lingo language, and the code samples listed here are called **chunk expressions**.

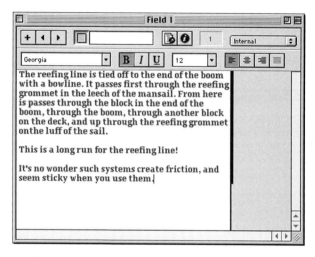

Figure 7.5 Text Field with Five Lines

You can use chunk expressions in Lingo scripts that include logical operators, such as the one below.

```
on mouseUp
    if field "mytextfield" contains field "searchword" then
        go to "found"
    else
        go to "notfound"
    end if
end mouseUp
```

The Lingo term `contains` means that the text in the second field appears somewhere in the first field. This is a looser match than `if    field "mytextfield" = field "searchword"`. The = term means that the text in the two fields must be identical.

Interacting with Text: An Example

To illustrate how you might use these kinds of functions and scripts in a Shockwave project, let's trace the development of one of the sections of the sample project described in earlier chapters. In this section, the user enters his name and then goes to a scene with a sailboat and an empty text field. Instructions tell him to type in the name of the sail that is highlighted. If he types the correct name, he goes on to the next sail. If not, he gets another chance. Also on the Stage is a text field that describes the parts of the boat. When the user clicks certain words in the text, the corresponding part of the boat highlights. The scene is shown in Figure 7.6.

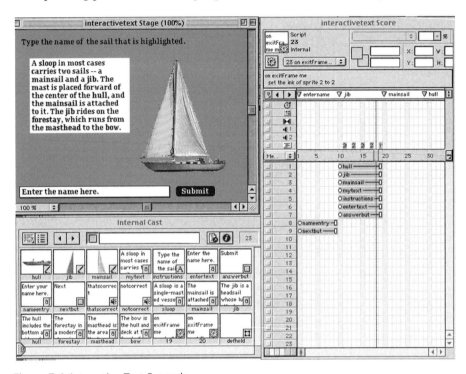

Figure 7.6 Interactive Text Example

Table 7.2 lists the items that make up this scene.

The Score for this exercise looks like Figure 7.7. Notice that there are four markers, one for the user to enter his name, then one for each part of the boat. The exercise begins in the first marker as the user enters his name in the field.

☆**TIP**   **Download This Sample Project**

To see this example in action, download the Director file from the Web Wizard's teacher support Web site. You can work through it as a user and examine the scripts, cast members, and Score.

Once entered, the string of characters that is the user's name remains in the field cast member `nameentry`. This way, you can use it later to address the user by name. But for now, the name will disappear from the Stage when the user clicks the button to go to the next marker.

Table 7.2 Items Used in the Interactive Text Example

Item	Cast Member Name	Sprite Number	Comment
Hull	`hull`	1	Paint cast member
Jib	`jib`	2	Paint cast member
Mainsail	`mainsail`	3	Paint cast member
Text passage	`mytext`	4	Field text, nine key words in blue
Instructions	`instructions`	5	Rich text
Text entry field	`entertext`	6	User-editable text field
Answer button	`answerbut`	7	Button cast member
Name entry field	`nameentry`	8	User-editable text field
Next button	`nextbut`	9	Button cast member
Correct voice	`thatscorrect`	None	Sound cast member
Incorrect voice	`notcorrect`	None	Sound cast member
Definitions of terms	Same as the words defined	12–18	Field text cast members, one for each key word in the text passage
Definition placeholder	`defhold`	21	Blank rectangle shape, on Stage but imperceptible

In this scene, the user sees the blinking jib and the instructions to enter the name of this sail into the text entry field at the bottom of the Stage. (The jib blinks because in the first frame of the scene its ink is set to `matte`, while in the second frame the ink is set to `ghost`.) The user enters a word and then clicks the answer button to submit his entry. The script on the answer button sprite checks the entry and acts accordingly.

```
on mouseUp
    if field "entertext" contains "jib" then
        puppetsound 1, "thatscorrect"
        put empty into field "entertext"
        go to "mainsail"
    else
        puppetsound 1, "notcorrect"
        put empty into field "entertext"
    end if
end mouseUp
```

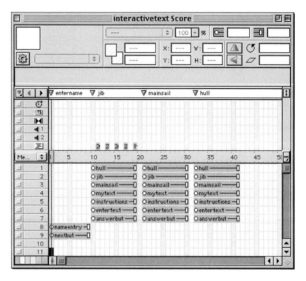

Figure 7.7 Score from the Sample Interactive Text Project

The reason for emptying the text entry field is to remove whatever the user typed before going to the next entry.

When the user clicks on a key word (colored blue) in the text passage, a script displays the definition of the word he clicked. Here's how the script on the text passage sprite looks.

```
on mouseUp
    if the forecolor of word (the mouseword) of field
            "textpassage" = "blue" then
        hilite word (the mouseword) of field "textpassage"
        set the member of sprite 21 to member (word (the
            mouseword) of field "textpassage")
    end if
end mouseUp
```

Since each key word in the text passage has a definition whose member name is the same as the word, this script replaces the blank placeholder rectangle in sprite 21 with one of the definition cast members.

Subsequent scenes contain the same kinds of scripts, modified slightly to fit the new content in that scene. In the final scene, the exercise concludes with the message, "Thank you for sailing with us, Jim." The Lingo script below places this message in a text field on the Stage.

```
on enterframe
    put "Thank you for sailing with us, "& field
            "nameentry"&"." into field "conclusion"
end
```

Enabling Text Functions with Lingo

◎◎ Interacting with Sound

You can use sound in three ways in a Shockwave project: in the sound channel, as a puppet sound, and in a sprite channel. The way you use a sound depends on the type of interactivity you wish to create.

Using the Sound Channel

This is the most common way to use sound. The sound, most often prepared in a program like SoundEdit 16, must first be imported into the Cast window. Then drag the sound from the Cast window into one of the sound channels in the Score, into the frames where you want the sound to occur. When Director plays the frames in which the sound appears, you will hear the sound. Make sure you extend the sound through enough frames so you can hear all of it—a 10-second sound will need to be dragged across 150 frames if you're running at 15 frames per second. (If you don't want to drag that far, you can select "wait for cue point . . . end" in the tempo channel of the Score, which will cause the Director movie to stay in that frame until the sound finishes playing.)

Using Puppet Sounds

In this method you import the sound into the Cast window as above, but you don't drag it into the Score. Instead, the sound is called forth and played from a Lingo script. For example, you could create a button that has the following script.

```
on mouseUp
   puppetsound 1, "mysoundname"
end mouseUp
```

Whenever the user clicks on this button, the sound plays through sound channel 1.

☆**WARNING Only One Sound Per Channel**

When you issue a `puppetsound` command to a sound channel, any other sound playing through channel 1 will be cancelled. If you want the playing sound to remain, aim the `puppetsound` command to a different channel (for example, `puppetsound 2`) and both sounds will play simultaneously.

Using a Sprite Channel

A sound can be a cast member like any other, imported into the Cast window and then dragged into any one of the regular sprite channels in the Score. To be used in this way, the sound must be saved in QuickTime (`.mov`) format. Use this method when you want to carefully synchronize visual events to the sound. When sound is in QuickTime format, it has a time code attached to it (regular sound does not). Shockwave can read this time code as the sound plays, and when it gets to a specific point, it can make other things happen. Use this method, for instance, to synchronize a word in a song to the appearance of a specific image on the Stage.

This synchronization requires a script like this one in the script channel of the Score.

```
on exitframe
   if the movietime of sprite 5 > 3456 then go to "nextpicture"
   go to the frame
end exitframe
```

The sound is in sprite channel 5. The `movietime` represents the number of **ticks** that have gone by since the beginning of the movie. A tick is one-sixtieth of a second. So in this example, the movie will go to the next marker about 58 seconds into the sound.

◎◉ Interacting with Video

You can include digital video in a Shockwave project and let the user interact with it, but you need to do this carefully, following certain filename conventions as you develop the project. The video can be in `.avi` or `.mov` format and can be on your own disk or on a video-streaming server. The instructions below cover QuickTime digital video, which allows more interactivity and can be streamed over the Web.

Preparing the Video

Save the video in the proper format, as described in Chapter Three. For best results with Shockwave, save the video in the `.mov` format, highly compressed, and in the "fast start" format. You can use QuickTime Player Pro or MovieCleaner Pro to export the video in this format. If the video will be streamed from a streaming server, copy the video to the streaming server now, and make a reference movie file on your own computer.

Save the video file in a folder on your computer called `dswmedia`. Shockwave can play videos from your computer only if they are in a folder with this name. (This is a security feature to prevent someone from making a Shockwave movie that when downloaded might alter files in other folders on a user's computer.) And when you save your `.dir` and `.dcr` files, it's a good idea to save them into this same folder.

Importing the Video into the Cast

Director will not actually incorporate the data from the movie into your project file. Instead, it will save a "pointer" to the video file on the disk, and when it needs the video it will get it from the disk. So once you import a video file, don't rename it or move it—Director will not be able to find it unless its name and location remain the same. The video will show up in the Cast window with a little QuickTime icon. Make sure the video is in the `dswmedia` folder before you import it.

Setting the Video's Properties

Double-click the video in the Cast window. This opens a window where you see the video full-size and can play it. Click on the little blue *i* button to see the video's properties. Here you can set the way it looks and plays. You can turn the sound on or off, have it come up playing or paused, loop it, or show its controller. Figure 7.8 shows the Property Inspector for a video cast member. The properties you choose will depend on how you want the video to appear on the Stage.

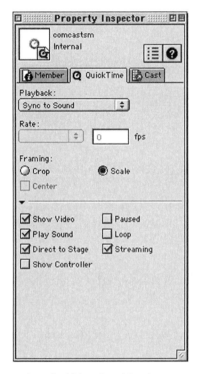

Figure 7.8 Setting the Properties of a Video Cast Member

The key property is the controller. Do you want to show the built-in controller under the video, which allows the user to play, stop, scan ahead, rewind, and adjust the volume? Or do you want to achieve control in other ways and display the video without the controller? A second important property is whether the video begins playing automatically or pauses at the first frame and waits for the user to play it.

Dragging the Video onto the Stage

Drag the video into one of the regular sprite channels, just like any other cast member. Place it on the Stage wherever you wish, but do not stretch or shrink the video—this will slow it down at playback time. And don't animate a video unless it is a very small one. Stretch the video across enough frames so that it has time to play. (Or use the tempo channel and select "wait for cue point . . .end" which will cause the Director movie to stay in that frame until the video finishes playing.)

Controlling the Video

You can issue scripts to control the video. The key Lingo terms are `movierate` and `movietime`. Let's suppose the video is in sprite channel 3.

☆ `set the movierate of sprite 3 to 1` starts the video playing at normal speed.

☆ `set the movierate of sprite 3 to 0` stops the video.

☆ `set the movierate of sprite 3 to 2` plays it twice the normal speed. (This does not work for streaming video.)

☆ `set the movierate of sprite 3 to -1` plays it backward. (This does not work for streaming video.)

☆ `set the movietime of sprite 3 to 1` rewinds the video to its beginning.

☆ `set the movietime of sprite 3 to 360` puts the video at 6 seconds from the beginning. (`movietime` is expressed in ticks. Each tick is one-sixtieth of a second.)

As with QuickTime sound files, you can use the timing of the video as it plays to make other things happen. The following script, for instance, waits for the movie to play for 10 seconds and then sends the Shockwave movie to the next marker, where appropriate text and images appear. A string of markers like this, with a video sprite that is carried across all of them, can present a synchronized set of video, text, and graphics.

```
on exitframe
    if the movietime of sprite 5 > 600 then go to "scene3"
    go to the frame
end exitframe
```

A video sprite is like an actor on the Stage who can appear, move, and speak and also be controlled by the audience. It's important that the video file that's in the **dswmedia** folder find its way to the Web server when your Shockwave project is posted to the Web. You'll learn more about this publishing and posting process in Chapter Eight.

◎◎ Interacting with Web Resources

Shockwave can interact with Web resources—you can let the user open a Web page from your Shockwave project, and you can embed Web resources into your Shockwave project. Here's how it's done.

Interacting with Web Resources

Opening a Web Resource

To link to a Web resource, use a script like the one below.

```
on mouseUp
   gotonetpage "http://www.bu.edu"
end mouseUp
```

This script opens the Boston University Web page in the user's browser. However, the Web page will replace your Shockwave project. So you might be better off using a script that opens the Web resource in a new window.

```
on mouseUp
   gotonetpage "http://www.bu.edu" , "new"
end mouseUp
```

This script opens the Boston University Web page in a new browser window, leaving your Shockwave project running in the original window.

☆ **SHORTCUT** **Copy and Paste URLs Instead of Typing Them**

When using URLs in your Lingo scripts, don't type them in from the keyboard—this often induces errors. Instead, open the URL in your browser, then select the URL from the location panel, copy it, go back to Director, and paste the URL into your script.

Not only Web pages can be linked—you can also allow access from Shockwave to a variety of Web resources such as:

☆ Images: `gotonetpage`
`"http://www.bu.edu/jlengel/cmc.gif", "new"`

☆ QuickTime movies: `gotonetpage`
`"http://www.bu.edu/jlengel/test.mov", "new"`

☆ PDF files: `gotonetpage`
`"http://www.bu.edu/jlengel/document.pdf", "new"`

☆ Other Shockwave projects: `gotonetpage`
`"http://www.bu.edu/jlengel/myshock.dcr", "new"`

Getting Cast Members from the Web

Suppose you want to include some timely material in your Shockwave project—dynamic materials that change over time, such as the current image from a Web cam or an up-to-date price list. You can include these as dynamic cast members that import themselves at the moment the user opens your Shockwave project.

For example, at `http://www.bristolyc.com/webcam/webcam.jpg` is an image that's updated every few hours, showing the current conditions at Bristol Harbor in Rhode Island. To use this image as a cast member in a Shockwave project, follow the steps below.

1. Choose Import from the File menu.

2. Click the Internet button on the right of the Import File dialog box.

3. Enter the URL of the Internet resource you want to import.

4. Click OK, and then click the Import button.

5. Watch the resource appear in the Cast window.

When your user opens the Shockwave project, it will download into its Cast window the current version of the resource from the Web. You can do the same with a text file on the Web, one that you post there yourself or one that's regularly posted by someone else. For instance, the Dean of the College of Communication at Boston University each day posts his summary of news relevant to communication professionals. It's posted daily at `http://www.bu.edu/COM/html/comnewstoday.html`. You can read this file; although it is an HTML file, it will be imported into Shockwave as a text cast member with the cast member name `comnewstoday`. Thus your user gets the latest version of the Dean's summary the moment she or he opens your Shockwave project. You could display for the user only the lead story by using a script such as the one below and setting up the Stage so that the field `leadstory` is displayed.

```
put member("comnewstoday").line[5..6] into field "leadstory"
```

☆TIP   **Citing Web Resources**

Give credit where credit is due. If you embed another person's work into your Shockwave project, as we did here with the Dean's news summary, make sure you credit the source, and if you need to, seek the author's permission. You should definitely seek permission if you copy and paste their work into your project.

◎◎ Creating Custom Cursors

When you move the mouse, what moves on the Stage is a black object shaped like an arrow. You can change this mouse cursor using Lingo commands in Director. This section explains how to design custom cursors and how to write scripts that control the new cursor in your project. There are two kinds of custom cursors: big colorful cursors and little black-and-white cursors.

Making Big Colorful Cursors

In this approach, you create a new cast member and use that cast member as the cursor. You could, for instance, replace the little arrow cursor with a life-size picture of a human hand. Or a basketball. Or a flashlight. Or a sailboat. Anything you can draw and place on the Stage as a sprite can become a cursor. Then you write a Lingo script that causes the picture sprite to follow the motion of the mouse. Here's how to do it, step by step.

1. Create your new cast member. The best results come with small cast members. You can import the cast member into the Cast window, draw it in the Paint

window, or copy and paste it from another source. If the cast member is in 32 bits or 16 bits, transform it in the Paint window to 8 bits (or even 4 bits, if it will take it). The smaller the cast member and the lower its color depth, the faster it will perform as a cursor.

2. Place your cast member into a sprite channel. Drag your new cast member onto the Stage as you would any other cast member. Put it in a high-numbered sprite channel, so that it appears in front of any other sprites on the Stage.

3. Write the "follow the mouse" script. The program must be in a go-to-the-frame loop for the custom cursor to work. The script in the script channel looks like this (assuming your custom cursor is in sprite channel 30).

```
on exitframe
    set the locH of sprite 30 to the mouseH
    set the lochV of sprite 30 to the mouseV
    go to the frame
end exitframe
```

4. Run the program and see if it works. As you move the mouse, the new cast member should follow it around the screen.

5. Make the old cursor disappear. Just before you go to the frame where the new cursor appears, issue this command in Lingo in the script channel.

```
on exitframe
    cursor 200
end exitframe
```

This causes the standard arrow cursor to disappear. Don't forget to make the arrow appear again when your custom cursor is finished, using this command.

```
on exitframe
    cursor -1
end exitframe
```

The numbers for some of the other standard cursors are 1 (I-beam), 2 (crosshair), 3 (crossbar), 4 (watch), and 280 (hand).

☆ **SHORTCUT Changing Cursors with the Behavior Inspector**

You can also create a cursor-change script using the Behavior Inspector. Select the object to which you want to attach the script, open the Behavior Inspector, create and name a new behavior, select the appropriate event (such as MouseEnter or Exitframe), and for the action choose Cursor→Cursor Change.

Making Little Black-and-White Cursors

Use this approach when you want a custom cursor that's very small (16 by 16 pixels) and has no color, only black or white, which allows it to be like an exact replacement for the arrow. You create a new cast member and then write a Lingo script that replaces the standard arrow cursor with the new one. Here are the steps.

1. Create your new cast member. Draw a new cursor in the Paint window or copy and paste it from another source. Make sure it is less than 16 pixels wide and 16 pixels high. When you are done, change the color depth (in the Paint window) to 1 bit. This reduces it to black and white. The cursor will not work unless it is a 1-bit paint object.

2. Use Lingo to change the cursor. Suppose your custom cursor is cast member 56. When you want the cursor to change, write the following Lingo command in the script channel.

```
on exitframe
    cursor [56]
end exitframe
```

This replaces the arrow with the custom cursor you just created. Don't forget to make the arrow appear again when your custom cursor is finished, using this command in a later frame in the script channel.

```
on exitframe
    cursor -1
end exitframe
```

Changing Cursors on Rollovers

This script changes the cursor only when the mouse rolls over a certain sprite.

```
set the cursor of sprite 5 to [56]
```

Or as an alternative, put this script on the sprite.

```
on mouseEnter
    cursor [56]
end mouseEnter

on mouseLeave
    cursor -1
end mouseLeave
```

Customizing the cursor lets you build in your Shockwave project an environment that simulates the real world and lets the user manipulate more than just an arrow.

◉◎ Keeping Score

Suppose you want to award points to the user of your Shockwave project whenever she accomplishes certain actions—every time she chooses the right answer, for instance, she gets five more points, and the score is continuously displayed on the Stage. An easy way to do this is to create a field text sprite on the Stage and name this field `"score"`. Then you can write a script that increments the number on the `"score"` field every time the user gets the answer right. The script, attached to the sprite that represents the correct answer, might look like the one below.

```
on mouseUp
    puppetsound 1, "correctsound"
    put value(field "score") +5 into field "score"
end mouseUp
```

And the script on the wrong answer sprite might look like this.

```
on mouseUp
    puppetsound 1, "wrongsound"
    put value(field "score") -5 into field "score"
end mouseUp
```

Looking Ahead

At this point, you should apply as many of these kinds of complex interactions as are appropriate to your Shockwave project. Try them: write scripts, modify scripts, and build the kinds of user control and feedback you need. Then test your project by showing it to others and letting them work through it while you're still in the Director environment, just as the playwright invites critics to the last rehearsals of the play. When your production is ready, go on to Chapter Eight and learn how to publish it.

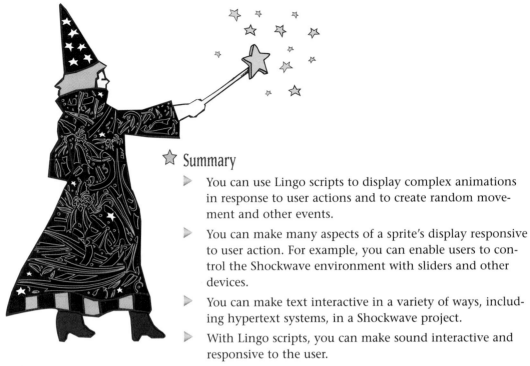

☆ Summary

▷ You can use Lingo scripts to display complex animations in response to user actions and to create random movement and other events.

▷ You can make many aspects of a sprite's display responsive to user action. For example, you can enable users to control the Shockwave environment with sliders and other devices.

▷ You can make text interactive in a variety of ways, including hypertext systems, in a Shockwave project.

▷ With Lingo scripts, you can make sound interactive and responsive to the user.

▷ You can also make video interactive with the help of scripting.

▷ Shockwave projects can embed Web resources such as text, graphics, and video. Shockwave projects can also link to Web pages and other Web resources.

▷ The appearance of the cursor can range widely to help create a more natural and interactive environment.

▷ Giving users feedback by including a score-keeping script can enhance your projects.

☆ Online References

Scripts 'n Lingo, a list of online Lingo scripting references
`http://www.mcli.dist.maricopa.edu/director/tips-script.html`

Lingo Forum on the Developer's Dispatch site
`http://developerdispatch.com/forums`

Update Stage, information and ideas for Director Developers
`http://www.updatestage.com/`

Director Online User Group
`http://www.director-online.com/`

Director Web, from Maricopa College, full of resources on building interactivity
`http://www.mcli.dist.maricopa.edu/director/`

☆ Review Questions

1. List the Lingo commands that modify each of these attributes of a sprite: transparency, size, position on the Stage, and rotation.

2. Explain how a repeat loop works and why you might use it in a Shockwave project.

3. List some attributes of the Shockwave environment that you might let the user control with a slider.

4. Explain at least three ways you can make text interactive in a Shockwave project.

5. What Lingo words are used to describe text in a field?

6. List at least two different ways you can make sound and video interactive in a Shockwave project.

7. How does Shockwave link to other Web resources, and how can you embed Web resources into a Shockwave project?

8. How could a custom cursor make a Shockwave project more interactive?

☆ Hands-On Exercises

1. Write four scripts, each making a modification in a different attribute of a sprite.

2. Write a script that uses Lingo's `random( )` function to create a change on the Stage.

3. Create an interactive exercise in which a sprite changes cast members in response to a user-initiated event.

4. Create a slider that lets the user control some aspect of the Shockwave environment.

5. Create an exercise that lets the user interact with text.

6. Include a sound or a video in a Shockwave project, and let the user interact with it in at least two different ways.

7. Create a Shockwave project that lets the user click a button that opens a particular Web page.

8. Create a custom cursor for your Shockwave project.

CHAPTER EIGHT

PUBLISHING YOUR PROJECT

What's done is done.
—from *Macbeth*

This chapter teaches you how to publish your project on the Web. It takes you through the process of testing your Director file and then creating a Shockwave file embedded in a Web page. After testing your Shockwave file, you will learn how to post your project to a Web server so that it is available to the world. Like the opening night for a theater production, this is an exciting event often approached with trepidation. Like many productions, your Shockwave project may not work properly when first published, so this chapter guides you through some troubleshooting suggestions. Since your production will find its venues on the display screens of many different computer users, you'll also have to take into consideration their capabilities and needs as you publish.

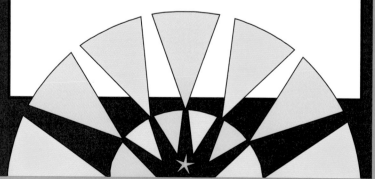

◎◎ Chapter Objectives

☆ To review and test your Director project so that it is ready for publication

☆ To create a Shockwave file from your project and test the file locally

☆ To post your project to a Web server and test it over the Web

☆ To learn how to make it easier for users to access your project

◎◎ Reviewing and Testing Your Project

Your project at this point is in Director format, with a `.dir` filename extension. Before turning it into a Shockwave file, you need to review the contents of your work, to make sure the file is as small as possible, and then to test your project for cross-platform compatibility.

Reviewing Your Project

Make sure your Stage size fits comfortably inside a browser window. If your Stage is more than 760 pixels wide and 450 pixels high, many users will have trouble seeing it on their computers. (It's a little late to change this now because changing the Stage size will in most cases require moving all the sprites.) Also make sure you have used no linked media except for digital video files and Internet (URL) resources, and make sure that the video files are in the same folder as your Director file.

Make the Director file as small as possible. For publishing on the Web, the file should be as small as you can make it. The two leading causes of large files are sounds and 32-bit paint cast members.

Reviewing Sound Cast Members

Check the size of the sounds in your project by selecting each one in the Cast window and then opening the Property Inspector. Under Member tab you will see the size of the sound in kilobytes, as shown in Figure 8.1.

The sound illustrated in Figure 8.1 is over 415KB, which for most users is too big for Shockwave—this sound alone would take about two minutes to download over a 56K modem. Reduce the size of your sounds by making them shorter or by compressing them as described in Chapter Three. You can achieve the best results by using Shockwave Audio compression (`.swa`), which you can accomplish with SoundEdit 16.

☆ **TIP**   **Finding Cast Members**

Can't locate your sound cast members easily in that crowded Cast window? Instead, choose Edit→Find→Cast Member from the menu bar. You will see a dialog box as pictured in Figure 8.2. Select the Type radio button, and then choose Sound from the pop-up menu. The numbers and names of all sound cast members will appear in the list. Double-click the one you want to inspect.

Figure 8.1 Reviewing the Size of a Sound Cast Member

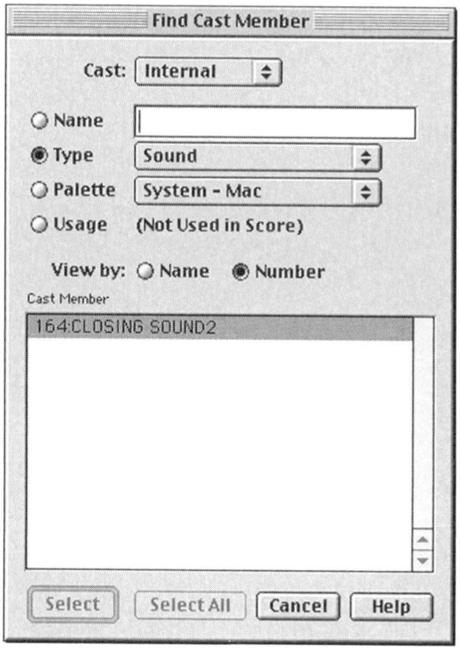

Figure 8.2 Finding Cast Members

☆ **WARNING External Sounds**

Certain capabilities of Director do not work on the Web with Shockwave. One of these is the playing of external sounds—those stored on the hard disk and played with the `sound playfile` command, rather than being imported into the cast. If you used any sounds this way, change them now by importing each sound into the Cast window and then using the `puppetsound` command in your scripts.

Reviewing Paint Cast Members

Open the Paint window and leaf through all your paint cast members by using the arrows at the top left of the window. Look down in the lower left of the window and observe the color depth of each cast member. If you find any 32-bit members, transform them to 16-bit members by double-clicking the color depth indicator and changing the value in the Transform Bitmap window (Figure 8.3). If they are not high-quality photographic images, reduce them further to 8 bits. This process can cut the cast member's size, and thus the download time, by as much as 75%.

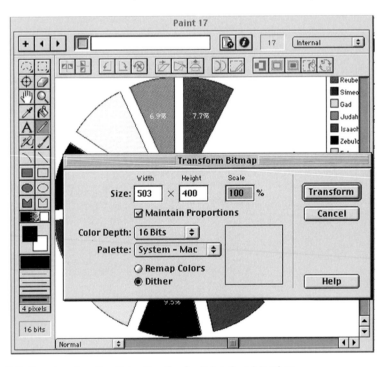

Figure 8.3 Transforming the Color Depth of a Paint Cast Member

Saving and Compacting Your Director File

Choose File→Save and Compact from the menu bar. This closes up any space you freed with your size reductions and saves an optimized `.dir` file. Check the size of this file. Estimate how long it will take for a user to download it with a 56K modem. Is your project worth that long a wait? If not, review your project again, looking for opportunities to reduce the size of cast members.

☆ SHORTCUT **Estimating Download Time**

A user on a 56K telephone modem will be able to receive data at about 3KB per second. Thus you can estimate the download time of your Shockwave file by dividing its file size in kilobytes by 3. This will result in a rough estimate of the number of seconds it will take to download. For example, a 240KB project will download in about 80 seconds, or 1 minute and 20 seconds.

Testing Your Project

Before creating the Shockwave file, you should test thoroughly your Director project while it is still in the `.dir` file format. Go through all the aspects of your project. Try out all the buttons, view all the animations, read all the text, listen to all the sounds. Let other people work through your project and watch them as they work. Make note of any changes you need to make. Change the things that need to be changed, and then test again.

If you created your project on a Windows computer, test it on a Macintosh, or vice versa. Note any anomalous findings. Some fonts may display differently on the other platform, and you may have to resize some of your text boxes. You will see some slight color differences, and some timing may be off. You need change only those things that make the project inoperable; it need not perform identically on both platforms.

☆ TIP **Cross-Platform Testing**

How do you test your project on the other platform? First you must locate a computer of the other type with Director installed. Then you must store your project on a medium that can be viewed from both sides, such as:

✲ A Windows-formatted Zip disk. These can be read on both platforms but require computers with Zip drives.

✲ A hybrid cross-platform CD-ROM. These require one computer with a CD-R drive and software that can create a true hybrid cross-platform CD-ROM, plus a CD drive on the second computer.

✲ A network server. The server must be one accessed by both the Macintosh and Windows computers on which you will test your project.

After you have put your project file on the test computer, open Director and run the project to see how it works on the other platform.

Once your project has been optimized and thoroughly tested on both platforms, you are ready to publish it in the Shockwave file format.

☆**WARNING** User Testing

It's a good idea to have typical users test your project. If you are the only reviewer, you may miss shortcomings. Set up your project on a computer and ask others who have never seen it to give it a thorough run-through. Watch them as they do it. In most cases, you will find several things you can improve.

Adding Xtras

If you used QuickTime movies, Flash animations, animated GIFs, or certain other file types in your Shockwave project, you will need to add the appropriate Xtras to your file. The Xtras provide the code necessary for the user's computer to interpret these file types. To add an Xtra, choose Modify→Movie→Xtras from the menu bar. Click the Add button, then choose the Xtra you need from the list.

◎◎ Creating a Shockwave File

Saving Your Shockwave File

Director makes it easy to publish your project in the Shockwave format and embed it into a Web page. It does this in a single step, but only if your publish settings are correct. Choose Publish Settings from the File menu, and then click the Default button in the dialog box (Figure 8.4). The default settings create a compressed Shockwave file, as well as a Web page with the Shockwave file embedded in it.

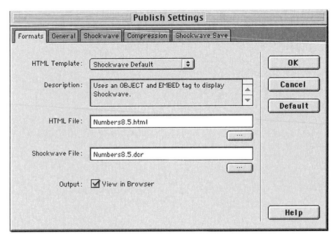

Figure 8.4 Publish Settings Dialog Box

When you are ready to publish, choose Publish from the File menu. Director will first create a Shockwave file with the `.dcr` filename extension and then create a Web page with the `.html` filename extension into which the Shockwave file has been embedded. These will be saved in the same folder as your Director file.

The Shockwave `.dcr` file will be smaller than the Director `.dir` file because it is compressed and because it has been stripped to the bone—it contains only the resources needed to play it back. All the resources needed to edit the project are removed. Thus you cannot open and edit the Shockwave `.dcr` file in Director—it has no Stage, no Score, no Cast or Script windows. If you find a mistake in the Shockwave file, you must discard it and make the repairs to the `.dir` file.

Embedding Shockwave into a Web Page

Director automatically generates the code that embeds your project into its Web page, and you need not concern yourself with the HTML. But for your information, the HTML code necessary to embed a Shockwave file into a Web page looks like that shown below.

```
<object classid="clsid:166B1BCA-3F9C-11CF-8075-
444553540000"
codebase="http://download.macromedia.com/pub/shockwave/
cabs/director/sw.cab#version=8,5,0,0"
   ID=myproject width=640 height=480>
<param name=src value="myproject.dcr">
<param name=swRemote value="swSaveEnabled='true'
swVolume='true' swRestart='true' swPausePlay='true'
swFastForward='true' swContextMenu='true' ">
<param name=swStretchStyle value=none>
<PARAM NAME=bgColor VALUE=#000000>

<embed src="myproject.dcr" bgColor=#000000  width=640
height=480 swRemote="swSaveEnabled='true' swVolume='true'
swRestart='true' swPausePlay='true' swFastForward='true'
swContextMenu='true' " swStretchStyle=none
   type="application/x-director"
pluginspage="http://www.macromedia.com/shockwave/
download/"></embed>
</object>
```

As you can see, this HTML code involves both <object> and <embed> tags, which seem redundant but are necessary if you want your project to work properly in the most recent versions of Microsoft Internet Explorer and Windows. The first part of the code sample provides the information necessary for the newer Windows Active-X media controls; the second provides the traditional code used for any source file that requires a browser plug-in. In both parts, the key aspects of this embedding are

☆ The *filename* of your project (`myproject.dcr` in this example)

☆ The *width* and *height* of the Stage (640 by 480 pixels here)

☆ The *URL* from which to download the Shockwave Player, which the user needs to display your project

Look at the source code of the HTML page that Director created for your project, and you will see a similar example.

☆TIP   Publish Settings

The instructions here use the default settings for creating the Shockwave .dcr file and embedding it into a Web page. Other settings are possible in the Publish Settings dialog box, such as adding HTML code in the Web page that detects whether the user has the Shockwave Player installed, using JPEG rather than Shockwave compression, stretching the Shockwave Stage to fit the user's browser window, and other possibilities.

Testing the Project Locally

Before posting your project to the Web for all to see, it's a good idea to test the Shockwave file on your own computer.

Testing Your Project in a Web Browser

Make sure you have the latest version of the Shockwave Player for your browsers. You can get the latest Shockwave plug-in from the Macromedia Web site at http://www.macromedia.com. Open the HTML file with your browser—from the browser's File menu choose Open File in Internet Explorer or Open→Page in Netscape Navigator. It should take a moment to load the Shockwave plug-in, then another moment to load the Shockwave file. If everything worked, you will see your project in the browser window.

Test the project to make sure it works. Test on both platforms, Macintosh and Windows, and in both browsers, Netscape and Explorer. That's four different tests. Go through the entire project, viewing every scene and clicking every button. Make note of anything that doesn't work.

☆WARNING   Linked Media Files

If your project accesses linked media files, such as digital videos, they must be in a folder named dswmedia, as explained in Chapter Seven. If your video doesn't work when you test it at this stage, look to make sure that it's in a dswmedia folder. Also, if your Shockwave project links to or embeds resources from the Web, you must be connected to the Web when you perform these tests.

Now go back to the Director .dir file and fix anything that doesn't work. Once fixed, you must publish again, creating new .dcr and .html files to replace the old.

☆ SHORTCUT   Publishing on CD-ROM

Shockwave projects were meant for the Web, but you can also distribute them on CD-ROMs. Simply burn onto a hybrid cross-platform CD-ROM the .html file, the .dcr file, and any digital video files linked to your project. The user then inserts the CD-ROM into her or his computer and double-clicks the .html file to launch your project.

◎◎ Posting Your Project to a Web Server

The audience for your Shockwave project will not be able to see it over the Internet until you post your project to a Web server. This section shows you how to do so.

If you built your project following the guidelines set forth in this book, it should work on most kinds of Web server: UNIX, Windows, or Mac OS X. You can also share it through most of the personal Web-sharing utilities available in the Windows and Macintosh operating systems.

Posting the Files

Copy your Shockwave project, consisting of the `.html` file, the `.dcr` file, and any linked media files, to a Web server. In most organizations, the Web master holds the keys to the Web server, and you need her or his permission to copy your files to the server. Some Web masters will ask for your files on disk or CD-ROM; some will give you a user name and password and let you send your files to the server by File Transfer Protocol (FTP); some will instruct you how to copy your files to the server over the Local Area Network (LAN).

In most cases, the Web master will set up a directory for your project. She or he will also assign you a user name and password that will allow you to copy files to that directory. No matter which method of posting you use, you need to copy all the files and folders from your project to the directory on the Web server. You must organize them on the Web server just as they are in your project folder—the directory structure must remain intact.

The Web master will also tell you the URL of your directory on the Web server. Through this URL you will test your posted project and users will be able to view it. The URL consists of the protocol, the server, the directory, and the file.

☆ *Protocol*: Shockwave projects use the Hypertext Transfer Protocol, so the URL will begin with `http://`.

☆ *Server*: The server will be indicated by its Internet Protocol (IP) address or by its domain name. Both of these are unique names that identify the Web server on the Internet. So this portion of the URL might take the form `128.197.190.100` or `www.bu.edu`.

☆ *Directory*: The server is divided into directories and subdirectories; the one assigned to you must be listed in the URL, in the form `/yourfiles/` or `/everybodysfiles/yourfiles/`.

☆ *File*: For this example, the file refers to the `.html` file you created earlier. It will be indicated in the URL in the form `myproject.html`.

So the URL for your Shockwave project might look like this:

`http://www.bu.edu/everybodysfiles/yourfiles/myproject.html`

Testing the Project on the Web

Once posted to a Web server, don't tell your audience the URL until you have tested to make sure your Shockwave project works correctly. Point your browser to the URL and watch what happens. The browser will load the Shockwave Player, then the Shockwave file, and then it will display your project in its window. Run through the project again. Follow the troubleshooting tips listed below, and then go back if necessary to the Director `.dir` file to make improvements. If you make any changes, you will need to repeat the publishing and posting processes described above.

Troubleshooting Your Project

Few Shockwave projects work perfectly in their first publication. Listed below are some common problems, along with suggested solutions.

Nothing Happens—Just a Blank Browser Window

The most likely cause is the absence of your Shockwave `.dcr` file on the Web server. When the `.html` file opens, it looks for the `.dcr` file. If it does not find it in its own folder, it simply presents a blank window. Check to see that your `.dcr` file is indeed sitting in the same folder as the `.html` file on the Web server and that its filename is correct.

The Browser Won't Load the File

In this situation you get an error message saying that the browser does not know how to handle the file of type application/x-director, with a request to save the file or to seek a plug-in. This is most often caused by an improper installation of the Shockwave Player or by the recent installation of another plug-in or player that overwrote the Shockwave installation. Reinstall the Shockwave Player.

The Browser Says It Needs the Player or Plug-in

This means that your browser does not have the Shockwave Player needed for your project. The solution is to download and reinstall the Shockwave Player. In most cases, you will be pointed automatically to the Macromedia download site.

The Project Takes Forever to Download

This means you have a very slow Internet connection, a very large Shockwave project, or both. The solutions are to get a faster connection, to reduce the size of your Shockwave file as described earlier in this chapter, or to do both.

The Project Doesn't Fit in the Browser Window

Your project's Stage size is too big, or the browser window is too small. Expand the browser window to fill the screen. Increase the number of pixels in your computer's display. If these actions don't fix the problem, go back to the `.dir` file and redesign your project with a smaller Stage size.

Sprites Don't Appear When They Should

The most likely cause is making a sprite channel invisible in an early part of the project and failing to make it visible later. Go back to the `.dir` file and check every time you use the `set the visible of sprite x to false` command, making sure that it's later rectified by a `set the visible of sprite x to true` command.

Sprites Appear When They Shouldn't

If you move a sprite off the Stage so it's not visible by using a script such as `set the loc of sprite x to point (-500, -500)`, this will work fine in Director but not in Shockwave—Shockwave can't manipulate space that's outside its rectangle in the browser window. A sprite pushed off the Stage under certain conditions will appear on the Stage when played in Shockwave. Use the `invisible` and `visible` commands instead to make sprites disappear.

The Video Won't Play

This is in most cases caused by an improper installation of the video player or plug-in. It is sometimes accompanied by a red X where the video was supposed to be. This problem can also arise if the video file is not in the correct directory on the Web server or if its filename has been changed since it was imported. The solution is to reinstall the latest version of the video player and check the location and filename of the linked video file.

Fonts Look Different

Fonts in field text sprites use the font files from the user's computer, which might not be identical to yours. You need not worry about this unless the user's fonts are larger in size. Then you may find that you need to make the field bigger to accommodate the text.

◎◎ Managing the User Experience

You don't want your audience to experience any of the situations described in the troubleshooting section above. You can prevent or minimize such unpleasant experiences by anticipating and precluding them. Here are some ways to ensure a pleasant user experience.

Let Users Know They Need Shockwave

In many cases, your Shockwave project will be linked from a Web page. It's a good idea to indicate that this link requires Shockwave, so that users will know what to expect. A simple addition of *"(Requires Shockwave.)"* after the link will be sufficient for most audiences.

Tell Them What They're Going to Get

To help users decide whether it's worth it to download Shockwave and wait for your project to arrive, provide on the referring page a short description of your project.

Point Them to the Shockwave Player

Even though the HTML code that embeds your Shockwave file into your Web page will automatically refer the user without Shockwave to the proper download site, it's still a good idea to provide a link from the referring page to the Shockwave download site. A simple hypertext link from the word *Shockwave* in the description of your project to `http://www.macromedia.com/shockwave/download/` is an easy way to accomplish this.

Let Them Know How Long They'll Have to Wait

An indication of the size of your project will help users decide whether to link to it. If they see a link such as *"My Great Project! (Requires Shockwave.) (67 MB),"* they might think twice before downloading it. Listing the file size is a courtesy to the user that can preclude disappointment.

Provide a Path for Feedback

Unlike the director and producer in the theater, you will probably never see your patrons—they will view your Shockwave project in the privacy of their desktops. So to gauge their reaction, it's a good idea to provide an e-mail link on the referring page, at the bottom of the HTML page that contains your Shockwave project, or inside the Shockwave project itself.

Thus, a complete link to a Shockwave project from a referring page might look like this:

> *Learn to Sail* with this interactive, hands-on introduction to the parts of a sailboat. Requires *Shockwave*. *566K. Send feedback to jlengel@bu.edu.*

Providing this information to the user in advance is like printing the poster for a theater production that tells the audience what to expect, provides information on the content, and indicates the extent of the work. Few people would go to the theater if they had no idea what they'd find there, or how long it would last, or whether or not they'd be able to understand the performance. Make your audience's experience with your Shockwave project easy and comfortable.

Congratulations! Your Shockwave production is now available to its audience. The results of your planning, preparing, casting, staging, and scripting are now available for interaction at any time, from any place.

Managing the User Experience

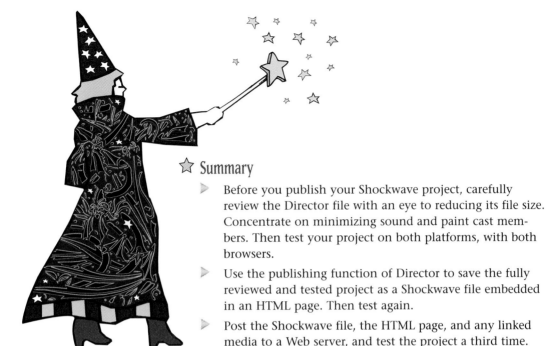

☆ Summary

> Before you publish your Shockwave project, carefully review the Director file with an eye to reducing its file size. Concentrate on minimizing sound and paint cast members. Then test your project on both platforms, with both browsers.

> Use the publishing function of Director to save the fully reviewed and tested project as a Shockwave file embedded in an HTML page. Then test again.

> Post the Shockwave file, the HTML page, and any linked media to a Web server, and test the project a third time.

> As you publish and post your project, consider the needs of users by providing specific information about your project on the referring Web page.

☆ Online References

Shockwave publishing instructions from Macromedia
`http://www.macromedia.com/support/director/internet.html`

Macromedia Shockwave Player Support Center
`http://www.macromedia.com/support/shockwave/`

Solving Shockwave Problems
`http://www.finearts.yorku.ca/nadine/multim/lingo/shockprobs.htm`

Tutorial on publishing a Shockwave file
`http://www.herts.ac.uk/lis/mmedia/directortutorial/animation8/publish.html`

☆ Review Questions

1. Why should you review sound and paint cast members one-by-one before publishing a Shockwave project?
2. List some ways you can reduce the sizes of sound and paint cast members.
3. How should you test the fully reviewed Director file?
4. Explain the importance of having someone other than yourself test your project.
5. Describe the process of publishing a Shockwave file from a Director file.
6. Explain two different methods for posting a Shockwave project to a Web server.

7. Describe at least three common problems that may require troubleshooting.

8. List some of the ways you can make the user's experience more comfortable.

☆ Hands-On Exercises

1. Review a Director file with an eye to reducing its size, examining and modifying cast members as necessary.

2. Test a Director file on both platforms and both browsers, making note of any anomalies.

3. Create a Shockwave file embedded in an HTML file, and test it with a browser.

4. Arrange with a Web master to post your Shockwave project to a Web server, and test the project over the Web.

5. Arrange your Shockwave project in a way that optimizes the user's experience.

APPENDIX: ANSWERS TO ODD-NUMBERED REVIEW QUESTIONS

Chapter One

1. Shockwave offers easy development of Web interactivity and animation with rich media.

3. The Shockwave Player ships automatically with most Web browsers and most new computers. Web users can also download it for free from the Macromedia Web site.

5. Lingo scripts enable you to build complex animation and interactivity. By attaching scripts to various objects in a Shockwave project, you can make it respond to the user's actions and to internal events.

7. The Flash player is smaller and somewhat more widely available than the Shockwave Player. Flash is best for vector graphic animation with limited activity. Shockwave is best for rich media with complex interactivity and logic.

Chapter Two

1. The list below names the main windows in Shockwave and their functions.
   - Stage window: Displays the project as the user will see it
   - Score window: Shows the flow of time and the distribution of sprites on the Stage
   - Cast window: Shows the various cast members of the project
   - Tool Palette: Provides tools for creating cast members
   - Control Panel: Lets the developer control the playing of the project

3. Director can import the following kinds of files.
   - Text prepared with a word processor such as Microsoft Word
   - Images prepared with an image editor such as Photoshop, in a variety of formats
   - Sound prepared with a sound editor such as SoundEdit 16
   - Video prepared with a video editing or playing program such as iMovie or QuickTime Player Pro
   - Vector graphics prepared with a program such as Adobe Illustrator or Macromedia Freehand
   - Animations prepared with Flash or in animated GIF format
   - Images created with a 3-D editor

5. Follow these steps to animate a sprite in the Score with path animation.

   a. Prepare the object to be animated and import it into the Cast window.

   b. Place the cast member onto the Stage at the beginning point of the animation.

   c. Stretch the sprite out in the Score for the proper number of frames.

   d. Click and drag the sprite's registration point across the Stage.

   e. Modify the path by selecting a frame in the Score and moving its point on the Stage.

   f. Test the animation by playing the movie.

7. You need scripts to get the project to respond to user actions and to create certain kinds of animation and interaction. Scripts can make things happen. Scripts provide logic and control for the Shockwave project. You write scripts in the Lingo scripting language and can attach them to sprites, cast members, frames, and the entire movie.

◎◎ Chapter Three

1. The key elements of a Shockwave project development plan include a statement of purpose, a definition of the audience, a list of the system requirements, an analysis of the competition, project structure, methods and design, a flow chart, a user walk-through, a budget, and a development schedule.

3. The flow chart illustrates the structure of the project, shows the flow of user activity through the project, helps define the needed media elements, and keeps track of marker and media elements names. The list of media elements provides organization and tracking of the developer's work in gathering and preparing the various files that will be imported into the Shockwave project.

5. To prepare an image file for importing into Director, follow the steps below.

   a. Compose the image in a form appropriate to the Web.

   b. Open it in an image editor, and set it to a size and resolution appropriate to its use in the project.

   c. Modify it as necessary to fit the needs of the project.

   d. Save it in a compressed format that Director can import.

7. File sizes are important because a Shockwave project needs to be as small as possible for transmission over the Web. Large file sizes translate into long download times for users.

◎◎ Chapter Four

1. To import a media element into Director, follow the steps below.

   a. Prepare and save the item in the proper format to your project folder.

   b. Choose Import from Director's File menu.

   c. Select the item in the Import dialog box, using Standard Import. (For files from the Internet, click the Internet button and enter the file's URL.)

   d. Import the item.

   e. Ensure that it appears in the Cast window.

3. Director's Paint window lets you create and edit bitmapped graphics. It contains tools for simple drawing, resizing, distorting, and changing the color depth of bitmaps, shapes, and text.

5. When designing the Stage for a Shockwave project, you must consider the needs of your project, the context in which it will appear, and the capabilities of your target users. Most Shockwave projects appear within a Web page and so need to be small enough to fit within the browser window along with the other elements of the page. The larger the page, the bigger the graphics, and the longer the download time. Size must also be matched to the target user's display resolution and browser window size.

7. Follow the steps below to put a cast member on the Stage.

   a. Create or import the cast member so it appears in the Cast window.

   b. Drag the item from the Cast window to the Stage or to a frame in the Score.

   c. Drag the item (now called a sprite) to its desired location on the Stage.

◎◉ Chapter Five

1. Path animation moves an object across the Stage, from one location to another, such as an airplane flying across the sky or a fish swimming in the sea. Parts-in-place animation moves the parts of an object that itself remains in the same location, such as a bird flapping its wings or a mouth moving.

3. Create a simple parts-in-place animation by following the steps below.

   a. Isolate the parts you want to move in the Paint window.

   b. Modify the parts in the Paint window, making each part a separate cast member slightly different from the next.

   c. Set the registration points of the various parts so they align properly.

   d. Arrange the moving parts on the Stage in the appropriate location, in adjacent frames.

   e. Set the ink of the parts' sprites to background transparent or matte as appropriate.

   f. Play the sequence of frames to test the animation, and modify accordingly.

5. Built-in behaviors are easy to choose and create and can accomplish complex animation effects with little scripting. However, these behaviors are difficult to modify and may conflict with other scripts that you may wish to attach to the sprite.

7. For effective animations, in most cases, animated sprites should be small, of low color depth, and used only where necessary. Text, shape, vector, and

bitmap sprites can all be animated. But animating too many at once may slow down the performance of the project. Lifelike animation takes skill and practice to create.

◎◎ Chapter Six

1. A Lingo script most often begins with an event handler, such as `on mouseUp` or `on exitframe`, followed by a series of commands, and ends with an `end` statement. Each command gets its own line in the script and can include various parameter settings (such as `set the locH of sprite 5 to 345`), logic tests (such as `if sprite 3 intersects 5 then go to "marker"`), or media commands (such as `puppetsound 1, "nicemusic"`).

3. The simplest navigation script is `go to "marker"`, which simply causes the playhead to jump to the marker and resume playing. Also used for navigation is `play "marker"`, which jumps to the marker and plays the frames until it encounters a `play done` command, at which point it returns to the frame from which it came.

5. Movement is most often accomplished by incrementally setting the location of the sprite, such as `set the locH of sprite 5 to (the locH of sprite 5) +10`. A sprite can be made to disappear by changing its visibility with a script such as `set the visible of sprite 5 to false` and to appear again with `set the visible of sprite 5 to true`.

7. You can adjust the tempo by using the tempo channel in the Score and choosing parameters in the Tempo dialog box. You can also change the tempo with a Lingo script such as `puppetTempo 15`.

◎◎ Chapter Seven

1. The sample commands below modify specific sprite attributes.
   - ✡ Transparency: `set the blend of sprite 5 to 50`
   - ✡ Size: `set the width of sprite 5 to 100, set the height of sprite 5 to 60`
   - ✡ Position: `set the locH of sprite 5 to 100, set the locV of sprite 5 to 100, set the loc of sprite 5 to point (100,100)`
   - ✡ Rotation: `set the rotation of sprite 5 to 180`

3. A slider can be used to control the volume of sound, the blend of a sprite, the position of a sprite, the playback rate of a QuickTime movie, the height or width of a sprite, a number in a field, the color of text, the size of text, the speed of an animation, and many other attributes.

5. The Lingo commands that deal with chunk expressions include `the mouseline`, `the mouseword`, `char`, `word`, `the forecolor`, `the backcolor`, `the hilite`, `the font`, `the fontSize`, `the fontStyle`, and many others. A Lingo script that modifies a single letter in a certain word in a text field might look like this: `set the fontStyle of char 1 of word 5 of line 6 of field "myfield" to "bold"`.

7. You can use the `gotonetpage` command to open a Web resource such as an HTML page or a Shockwave movie. Import Web resources into a Shockwave project as cast members by choosing Import from the File menu, clicking the Internet button, then entering the URL of the Web resource. When the project loads into the user's browser, Shockwave goes out on the Web, gets the resource, and puts it into the Cast window.

◎◎ Chapter Eight

1. Since sound and paint cast members are in most cases the largest elements in your Shockwave project, they often keep the file size too large for easy downloading. By examining these cast members one-by-one, you have a chance to modify their size, length, compression ratio, sampling rate, or color depth to make them and thus the entire project smaller.

3. You should test the fully reviewed Director file on both platforms (Macintosh and Windows) and at the display size of your target user. You should go through every part of the project, testing every possibility and every interaction. Test it yourself, but also have others, especially members of the target audience, test it.

5. Follow the steps below to publish a Shockwave file from a Director file.
   a. Test your Director file thoroughly.
   b. Make sure your publish settings are correct, which in most cases means using the default settings.
   c. Choose Publish... from the File menu, and watch Director create the Shockwave (`.dcr`) file and then the Web page (`.html`) file into which the Shockwave file is embedded.
   d. Open the Web page in your browser to test the Shockwave project.

7. The following are common problems that may require troubleshooting.
   ✣ The Shockwave project does not appear because the user lacks the Shockwave Player.
   ✣ The project takes a long time to download because it is too big or because the user's connection to the Internet is too slow.
   ✣ Certain elements do not appear because the user lacks the plug-in (sound or video) or because you made the sprite channel invisible at some point and didn't return it to the visible state.

INDEX

CREDITS

Figure 1.1   http://www.timex.com/flash/rushSIMULATION.html, reproduced courtesy of Timex Corporation

Figure 1.2   http://farfar.2038.com/english/loader.html

Figure 1.4   http://www.msnbc.com/modules/rainforestSimulation/

Figure 2.1   Reproduced courtesy of Macromedia.

Figure 2.2   Reproduced courtesy of Coppelia Music Publishing, 83 Timberline Drive, Nanuet, New York 10954. Composer: Pietro Ayon, Arranger: Lawrence Keith Zaidan